CityPack
Montréal

TIM JEPSON

*Tim Jepson's love of travel
began with a busking trip
through Europe and has taken
him from the Umbrian
countryside to the Canadian
Rockies and the windswept
tundra of the Yukon. Future
plans include walking the
length of Italy and exploring
the Arctic and South America.
Tim has written several books
for the AA, including Explorer
guides to* Canada, Rome,
Italy, Florence & Tuscany
and Venice. *Other publications
include* Rough Guides *to*
Canada *and* The Pacific
Northwest.

City-centre
map continues
on inside back
cover
←

AA Publishing

Contents

About this book 4

best 49–60

where to... 61–86

travel facts 87–93

About this book

KEY TO SYMBOLS

🛉 map reference on the fold-out map accompanying this book (see below)

📧 address

☎ telephone number

🕓 opening times

🍴 restaurant or café on premises or nearby

🚇 nearest Métro (underground) train station

🚉 nearest railway station

🚌 nearest bus route

⛴ nearest riverboat or ferry stop

♿ facilities for visitors with disabilities

✋ admission charge

↔ other nearby places of interest

❓ tours, lectures or special events

➤ indicates the page where you will find a fuller description

ℹ tourist information

CityPack Montréal's six sections cover the six most important aspects of your visit to Montréal. It includes:

- Montréal – the city and its people
- Itineraries, walks and excursions – how to organise your time
- The top 25 sights to visit – arranged from west to east across the city
- Features about different aspects of the city that make it special
- Detailed listings of restaurants, hotels, shops and nightlife
- Practical information

In addition, text boxes provide fascinating extra facts and snippets, highlights of places to visit and invaluable practical advice.

CROSS-REFERENCES

To help you make the most of your visit, cross-references, indicated by ➤ , show you where to find additional information about a place or subject.

MAPS

The fold-out map in the wallet at the back of the book is a comprehensive street plan of Montréal. All the map references given in the book refer to this map. For example, the Musée des beaux-arts on rue Sherbrooke-Ouest has the following information: 🛉 **E8** indicating the grid square of the map in which the Musée des beaux-arts will be found.

The city-centre maps found on the inside front and back covers of the book itself are for quick reference. They show the top 25 sights, described on pages 24–48, which are clearly plotted by number (**❶** – **㉕**, not page number) from west to east.

MONTRÉAL
life

INTRODUCING MONTRÉAL

Top city

Montréal is one of the world's most agreeable places to live, according to a survey of the world's largest 100 urban areas by Population Action International in Washington DC. The city is also the gastronomic capital of Canada, rated North America's second-best city for eating (after New York) by both the American and Canadian automobile associations (AAA and CAA).

Montréal's impressive skyline, bisected by rue Sainte-Catherine

Montréal is Canada's second biggest city, the only French-speaking metropolis in North America and – after Paris – one of the largest French-speaking cities in the world. Situated at the heart of the St Lawrence River, on one of over 230 river islands, it juxtaposes a centre of gleaming sky-scrapers with an old quarter of narrow, cobbled streets and 18th- and 19th-century buildings. Museums, churches and galleries abound; the city has plenty of parks, a rejuvenated harbour area, and several superbly atmospheric quarters crammed with bars, cafés and fine restaurants.

The city itself is fairly easy to navigate. The streets are laid out in a grid and most of the important sights, best restaurants and trendiest night spots are clustered around the foot of Mont-Royal, the 233-m high green knoll that rises above the downtown area. The rest are easily accessible by Métro. There is one com-plication, however: Montréalers determine direction not by the compass but by the river. Upstream is always west, downstream is always east, and it makes no difference that the river actually flows north as it rounds the island. Streets that run perpendicular to the river are

said to run from north to south, with their numbers starting low by the river and increasing away from it; those that run parallel to it are said to run from east to west; all numbers start at boulevard Saint-Laurent (known as The Main or Le Main), and climb as you go 'east' or 'west'.

Irresistibly, most visitors head straight for Vieux-Montréal, the heart of the historic city, a small but enticing enclave of old streets along the St Lawrence River. The centre of Montréal fills the area 'north' of the old city and creeps up the lower slopes of Mont-Royal. Its two main shopping streets, rue Sherbrooke and rue Sainte-Catherine, bustle with life, but it also encompasses the leafy green campus of McGill University. City nightlife is centred on small side streets like rues Crescent, de la Montagne and Bishop.

Houses in the Saint-Louis district

The Main, a little 'east' of the main core, is rich in restaurants and nightclubs, as is rue Saint-Denis, which runs through the vibrant Quartier Latin. 'North' of rue Sherbrooke is Plateau Mont-Royal, one of the city's liveliest and most ethnically diverse neighbourhoods – Greek, Portuguese and East-Asian among others – filled with restaurants and clubs. Montréal's gay area, known simply as Le Village, is centred on rue Sainte-Catherine Est between rue Amherst and Avenue Papineau.

'East' of The Main is still predominantly French; the centre and the 'west' more firmly English. These days – with French speakers in a four to one majority – the sense of the entire city is French, though most people are bilingual. It is Montréal's French influences and traditions that give the city its appeal. The Old-World charm in a North American context produces not only a sophisticated and cosmopolitan air – apparent in the city's restaurants and European-style café-life – but also the idiosyncratic character that makes the city so alluring.

Famous locals

William Shatner, better known as Captain James T Kirk of *Star Trek's* USS Enterprise, hails from Montréal, as do jazz musician Oscar Peterson, novelist Mordecai Richler, and poet and musician Leonard Cohen, who can sometimes be seen in the bars and restaurants off boulevard Saint-Laurent. Pop diva Céline Dion, born in nearby Répentigny, calls Montréal home.

A DAY IN THE LIFE OF A MONTRÉALER

While Montréal is predominantly French, it is home to many other ethnic groups. Yet certain pleasures seem common to all, year round.

Love of food, in a variety of styles, is one of the most obvious. Breakfast is either the coffee and croissant of far-away France, the humble Canadian muffin, or a full bacon-and-egg extravaganza sometimes with regional additions like baked beans and toast spread thickly with *cretons* (a kind of coarse, fatty pâté made from pork). Lunch is a bistro meal, a snack in a mall or an expense-account feast. Dinner, usually eaten at about 8PM, can be enjoyed in any one of the city's 4,000 or more restaurants. Montréalers pride themselves on their gourmet tastes, but they can get passionate over humble fare as well. Local favourites include steamed hot dogs (*stimés* in local parlance), bagels (the best ones are baked at Fairmount Bagel Factory), and, of course, smoked meat – beef brisket prepared according to a recipe imported by Romanian Jews early in the century (no one serves a better version of this delicacy than Schwartz's).

Nightlife is another shared passion. Do as Montréalers do, and eat, drink and talk late, then round off the evening with one of those famous bagels. Bars stay open until 3AM and beyond, and 5AM traffic jams are not unknown on boulevard Saint-Laurent.

On cold winter days, Montréal families go tobogganing or cross-country skiing on Mont-Royal, and those lucky enough to get tickets watch the Canadiens take on the best of the National Hockey League at the Molson Centre. In spring, join the locals in sampling the season's first maple syrup. During the summer follow them to the beach on Île Notre-Dame, revel with them at one of the city's festivals, or at a Montréal Expos baseball game in the Olympic Stadium. Walk along rue Sainte-Catherine on any Saturday morning to see city shoppers in action. Most important, sit at a pavement café and watch the world go by – everybody else does.

Brightly lit rue Sainte-Catherine enticingly beckons

Winter

For sheer destruction, few storms can match the ice storm of January 1998 that plunged Montréal into darkness for more than a week. The worst snowstorm hit the city on 4 March 1971, with 90kph winds dropping 43cm of snow in 24 hours and another 18cm following three days later. This was also the snowiest winter, with a total of nearly 4m of snow. The lowest average temperature recorded over December, January and February was in 1902–3, when it hit -12.5°C.

MONTRÉAL IN FIGURES

Geography
- Latitude: 45° N – the same as Venice
- Longitude: 73° W – the same as Concepción, Chile
- 253km from Québec City; 608km from New York; 6,100km from London
- Distance from the Atlantic Ocean: 1,600km
- Average temperature in January: maximum -5.7°C, minimum -14.6°C
- Average temperature in July: maximum 26°C, minimum 15.6°C
- Average annual snowfall: 242cm

People
- Population: 1,806,754 (1998)
- Percentage with French as first language: 68.6 per cent
- Percentage with English as first language: 13.3 per cent
- Percentage with other mother tongues: 18.1 per cent
- Number of ethnic groups: more than 32
- Percentage aged 20–44: 44 per cent

City
- Number of visitors annually: over 5 million
- Kilometres of Métro track: 64.4
- Average number of daily passengers: 1 million
- Number of bus routes: over 150
- Kilometres of cycleways: over 108
- Kilometres of underground passageways: 29

A busy restaurant in Place Jacques-Cartier

A CHRONOLOGY

1535   French explorer Jacques Cartier is the first European to set foot on the site of Montréal, and is welcomed by the Iroquois of Hochelega. Cartier names the island's hill Mont-Royal.

1556   Italian writer G B Ramuso translates Mont-Royal as Mont-Real.

1611   Frenchman Samuel de Champlain sets up a trading post called Place Royale.

1642   Paul de Chomedey, Sieur de Maisonneuve, a French soldier, establishes Ville-Marie on the island of Montréal at the confluence of the Ottawa and St Lawrence rivers. He is helped by the indomitable Jeanne Mance.

1663   King Louis XIV awards land rights on the Île de Mont-Réal to the Sulpicians, a religious order trying to convert the native population, aided by Marguerite Bourgeoys.

1682   The Compagnie du Nord makes Ville-Marie a major fur-trading centre. The company trades with France's Algonquin and Huron allies; its rival is the Hudson's Bay Company – English merchant adventurers trading with the natives on all territories draining into Hudson Bay.

1701   The French end their 50-year struggle with the powerful Iroquois Confederacy, enemies of France's Algonquin and Huron partners.

1710   The name Ville-Marie is dropped.

1756   The Seven Years' War breaks out between England and France.

1759   The British defeat the French in Québec.

1763   The Treaty of Paris ends the Seven Years' War.

1775   American revolutionary troops occupy Montréal in an effort to enlist French Canadians to their cause.

1792	Immigration from Ireland and Scotland drives Montréal's population up to 6,000. British merchants form the North West Company, a rival to the Hudson's Bay Company.
1825	The Lachine Canal is completed, allowing ships to travel from the Atlantic to the Great Lakes.
1832	Montréal is incorporated as a city, becoming North America's second largest metropolis.
1844	Montréal becomes the capital of the newly formed United Province of Canada, which joins Lower and Upper Canada.
1867	The Dominion of Canada is established, consisting of Québec, Ontario, New Brunswick and Nova Scotia.
1886	The Canadian Pacific Railway links Montréal to the Pacific coast and the city develops into the financial and industrial capital of Canada.
1940	Colourful mayor Camillien Houde is interned after urging young Canadians not to register for wartime conscription.
1959	The St Lawrence Seaway opens.
1967	Expo '67 – a world fair celebrating Canada's centennial – attracts 53 million visitors.
1969	The Official Languages Act recognises both French and English as official languages.
1976	Montreal hosts the summer Olympic Games.
1977	Bill 101 makes Québec a monolingual Francophone province. Around 100,000 English-speakers leave Montréal.
1995	Barely 50 per cent of Québécois vote to remain part of Canada in a referendum.
1998	Freak January ice storm brings the city to a standstill for more than a week.

PEOPLE & EVENTS FROM HISTORY

The man who gave Montréal its name

JACQUES CARTIER

Norman seaman Jacques Cartier (1491–1557) was looking for a route to China when he set foot on what is now Montréal in 1535. The Lachine Rapids stopped him, but he did claim the Gaspé Peninsula in the name of King Francis I of France. He fell out of favour after a third voyage up the St Lawrence, when the 'gold and diamonds' he returned with turned out to be iron pyrites and quartz.

PAUL DE CHOMEDEY, SIEUR DE MAISONNEUVE

Paul de Chomedey de Maisonneuve (1612–76), a pious soldier with dreams of establishing an idealistic Christian society, is credited with founding Montréal. He and 53 followers landed on the island in 1642 and established a small settlement on Pointe-à-Callière, which they named Ville-Marie in honour of Christ's mother. Before the year was out, the community barely survived a severe flood, and de Maisonneuve showed his gratitude by carrying a wooden cross to the summit of Mont-Royal. He proved to be an excellent leader, ensuring that the colony was both well-defended and well-founded in farming, business and law. He was recalled to France in 1665 and lived out his life in seclusion in Paris.

JEANNE MANCE

The co-founder of Montréal was the indomitable Jeanne Mance (1606–73), a pious, strong-willed French woman who had been interested in foreign missions since girlhood. She never married or joined a religious order, but she built Montréal's first hospital, Hôtel-Dieu (► 51), and recruited Marguerite Bourgeoys to found the city's first school. She died in Montréal at the age of 67 and was buried in the church of the Hôtel-Dieu which was destroyed in a fire in 1696. In 1861, the hospital was transferred to the foot of Mont-Royal and stands next to the park bearing her name.

Marguerite Bourgeoys

Bourgeoys landed at Montréal with de Maisonneuve in 1642. A vision shortly after her arrival inspired her to build the Chapelle Notre-Dame-de-Bonsecours, a shrine to the Virgin outside the settlers' original stockade. She became Canada's first school-teacher and founded the Congrégation de Notre-Dame, Canada's first order of non-cloistered nuns. Canonised in 1982, she is the first saint to have lived and died in Canada.

MONTRÉAL

how to organise your time

ITINERARIES

To get the most out of a short visit, concentrate on a few sights in one or two of Montréal's more well-defined districts.

ITINERARY ONE	DOWNTOWN
Morning	All visits to Montréal should start at the top of Mont-Royal (➤ 27) for a panoramic view of the city. Follow the footpaths down to avenue des Pins and then continue to McGill University (➤ 29). Stroll through the campus to the McCord Museum of Canadian History (➤ 30) and spend the rest of the morning viewing the vast array of eclectic exhibits.
Lunch	Picnic on the campus or try the food courts at the Centre Eaton (➤ 76) and browse amongst its five floors of shops.
Afternoon	Start with a quiet moment in Christ Church Cathedral (➤ 33) and then descend into the shops of the Promenades de la Cathédrale and the Underground City (➤ 34). Work your way through the malls and tunnels to Place Ville-Marie (➤ 55), browsing in the boutiques as you go. Emerge for a look at the Cathédrale Marie-Reine-du-Monde (➤ 35) and walk along boulevard René-Lévesque Ouest to St Patrick's Basilica (➤ 37).
ITINERARY TWO	VIEUX-MONTRÉAL
Morning	Start early at the Basilique Notre-Dame (➤ 38) for a moment's calm before the tour buses disturb the morning peace. Then walk along rue Notre-Dame to Place Jacques-Cartier (➤ 52) to admire the view of the Vieux-Port de Montréal. Visit the 18th-century Château Ramezay (➤ 41) and then continue to the Lieu historique national Sir-George-Étienne-Cartier (➤ 42). Retrace your steps to rue Bonsecours (➤ 57) and then head towards the waterfront to the attractive Chapelle Notre-Dame-de-Bonsecours (➤ 43) and on to Marché Bonsecours, the graceful market building with its distinctive dome (➤ 44).

Lunch	Choose a pavement café on Place Jacques-Cartier or eat a picnic lunch on the square.
Afternoon	Walk along rue Saint-Paul to Place Royale (► 52) and the archaeological museum at Pointe-à-Callière (► 40). Plan at least an hour there and another half an hour at the nearby Centre d'histoire de Montréal (► 39).

ITINERARY THREE — WATERFRONT AND ISLANDS

Morning	Stroll the length of the Vieux-Port de Montréal (► 45) downriver ending up at the Clock Tower for a grand view of the waterfront. Retrace your steps to the Quai King-Edward for a visit to the iSci science centre.
Lunch	Picnic in the Vieux-Port or try one of the many pavement cafés along rue de la Commune.
Afternoon	Hire a bike and then catch the ferry to Île Sainte-Hélène (► 46) for an afternoon of riding through open parkland. Visit the Old Fort; look at the exhibition on the environment at the Biosphère (► 47) and view the city from its observation deck; stroll through the flower gardens and relax on the beach on Île Notre-Dame (► 48).

ITINERARY FOUR — ARTS AND FLOWERS

Morning	Spend an hour wandering through the Musée d'art contemporain (► 36) near the Place des Arts and then take the Métro to the Pie-IX station and visit the Biodôme (► 24). After a ride to the top of the Olympic Tower (► 25) it will be time for lunch.
Lunch	Restaurant choices are not numerous in these outskirts of town, so try the lunch room in the Biodôme or picnic in the Parc Maisonneuve (► 56).
Afternoon	Take the free shuttle bus to the Jardin botanique (► 26) and spend a full afternoon visiting the gardens and the Insectarium.

WALKS

In the basement kitchen of the Château Ramezay

INFORMATION

Distance 3km
Time 2–6 hours
Start point Place Jacques-Cartier
🚇 G7
🚊 Champ-de-Mars
🚌 7
End point Place Jacques-Cartier
🕐 Most sights are open all day
🍴 Vieux-Montréal is well provided with cafés, bars and restaurants.

PLACE JACQUES-CARTIER AND VIEUX-MONTRÉAL

Start at the Infotouriste building at Place Jacques-Cartier and rue Notre-Dame Est. The statue on the column is not of French explorer Jacques Cartier but of Admiral Lord Horatio Nelson, and was erected after his victory over the French fleet at Trafalgar in 1805. Turn left up rue Bonsecours past the Maison du Calvet and Maison Papineau to the Lieu historique national Sir-George-Étienne-Cartier. Then walk towards the port on rue Berri and turn right onto rue Saint-Paul for the Chapelle Notre-Dame and Marché Bonsecours.

From rue Saint-Paul turn right onto rue Saint-Claude and then left at rue Notre-Dame to see the Château Ramezay. Continue along rue Notre-Dame and turn left into Place Jacques-Cartier. Turn right halfway down the square onto rue Saint-Amable. At its end, turn left, then right; follow rue Saint-Paul across boulevard Saint-Laurent. At rue Saint-Sulpice turn right to reach the Place d'Armes and the Basilique Notre-Dame.

Walk south down rue Notre-Dame Ouest and take the first left, rue Saint-François-Xavier (note the old Stock Exchange at No. 453), now the home of Centaur, Montréal's leading English-language theatre. Cross rue Saint-Paul into the Place Royale to see Pointe-à-Callière. Then walk south past the Founders' Obelisk to the Place d'Youville.

From in front of the Centre d'histoire de Montréal walk east on rue Saint-Pierre towards the waterfront. Cross rue de la Commune and the railway tracks and then turn left to follow the grassy waterfront area past the lake and Vieux Port back to Place Jacques-Cartier.

DOWNTOWN AND
BOHEMIAN RUE SAINT-DENIS

Each of the two areas on this long walk could fill
an entire day. Striking modern buildings include
Édifice IBM-Marathon, Maison Alcan, Tour BNP-
Banque Laurentienne (all ► 55) and the Promenades de la Cathédrale mall (► 77) – in sharp
contrast with Square Saint-Louis (► 53).

Begin at the Bonaventure Métro station and
walk through Place du Canada and Square-
Dorchester. Turn right at rue Sainte-Catherine
and left onto avenue McGill College, a short
street lined with office towers and shopping
malls, with a fine view of Mont-Royal and the
McGill University campus. Turn right onto
boulevard de Maisonneuve and right again to
avenue Union to see Christ Church Cathedral.

Turn left onto rue Sainte-Catherine, one of
Montréal's main shopping streets, and follow it
past the Musée d'art contemporain to boulevard
Saint-Laurent. Turn left onto the boulevard,
leaving plenty of time for the shops and any side
streets that take your fancy. Turn right at the
pedestrian rue Prince-Arthur Est. Ethnic
restaurants – mainly Greek and East
Asian – abound here. Most allow you
to bring your own alcohol.

For a real taste of Montréal, however,
walk a dozen blocks north on
boulevard Saint-Laurent
and order yourself a
smoked-meat sandwich
(medium lean) at Schwartz's, the
best and busiest deli in town.
Next, follow rue Prince-Arthur
through Square Saint-Louis. If
time allows turn left at rue Saint-
Denis and explore the charming
streets around rue Roy and
rue Duluth. Otherwise
turn right and walk
down to the lively
Quartier Latin.

THE SIGHTS

- Mont-Royal (► 27)
- McGill University (► 29)
- Christ Church Cathedral
  (► 33)
- Musée d'art contemporain
  (► 36)

INFORMATION

Distance 5km
Time 2–4 hours
Start point Square-Dorchester
🚇 F8
🚊 Bonaventure
End point Berri-UQAM Métro
🚇 F6
🕐 Most sights open all day

*A memorial in Square-
Dorchester to the
Canadians who died
in the South
African war*

GEO. W. HILL

17

EVENING STROLLS

Place Jacques-Cartier

INFORMATION

Distance 1km
Time 15–20 minutes
Start point Place d'Armes
➕ G7
🚇 Place-d'Armes
🚌 38 to Place d'Armes
End point Place Jacques-Cartier
➕ G7
🚇 Champ-de-Mars
🚌 38

INFORMATION

Distance 2km
Time 45 minutes–1 hour
Start point Square Saint-Louis
➕ F6
🚇 Sherbrooke
🚌 24 to rue Saint-Denis
End point Square Saint-Louis or
Théâtre Saint-Denis
➕ F6
🚇 Sherbrooke or Berri-UQAM

VIEUX-MONTRÉAL

Start your outing in Place d'Armes, pausing to admire the Basilique Notre-Dame, and then wend your way south until you come to Place d'Youville. Cut down to the Centre d'histoire de Montréal before returning to rue Saint-Paul and follow this north until you come to rue Saint-Vincent. Turn left here and then right onto rue Saint-Amable and Place Jacques-Cartier.

SQUARE SAINT-LOUIS

This is the heart of Montréal's liveliest restaurant and nightclub districts, a bustling mass of gourmet restaurants, cafés, bars, fast-food outlets, ethnic eateries with bring-your-own bottle policies, bookshops and delis. Much of the action is north of rue Sherbrooke, and a good place to start is at the very elegant Square Saint-Louis. Walk along rue Prince-Arthur, the square's southern boundary, to boulevard Saint-Laurent and turn right. Work slowly through the crowds to rue Duluth and rue Rachel. Double back on either of these shop-and-restaurant-lined streets to rue Saint-Denis and then back towards the river to Square Saint-Louis. If there's time, you can continue past rue Sherbrooke to the only slightly less lively area that surrounds the Théâtre Saint-Denis.

ORGANISED SIGHTSEEING

BUS TOURS

Gray Line Nine different Montréal coach tours in summer (one in winter).

🚇 F7 ✉ Tickets: Infotouriste, 1001 Square-Dorchester ☎ 934 1222 🕐 May–Sep: daily 7AM–8PM; Oct–Apr: daily 9–5 🚾 Peel

Autocar Royal Tour the city on a trolley bus.

🚇 F7 ✉ Tickets: Infotouriste, 1001 Square-Dorchester ☎ 871 4733 🕐 May–Sep: daily 7AM–8PM; Oct–Apr: daily 9–5 🚾 Peel

Amphi-Bus Tours the streets and then takes to the water.

🚇 G7 ✉ rue de la Commune at boulevard Saint-Laurent ☎ 849 5181 🚾 Place d'Armes

La Balade Bilingual 45-minute mini-bus tours cover the Vieux-Port area in summer.

🚇 G7 ✉ Quai Jacques-Cartier ☎ 496 PORT 🚾 Place d'Armes

Calèche Horse-drawn carriages – expensive but fun – go for hour-long rides from Square-Dorchester, Place Jacques-Cartier, Place d'Armes or rue de la Commune.

🚇 F7–G7 ☎ 934 6105 🚾 Bonaventure, Place d'Armes

BIKE TOURS

Vélo-Tour Montréal Two-wheeled tours in French, English or Spanish.

🚇 G7 ✉ 99 rue de la Commune Ouest ☎ 236 8356

Vélo Adventure Montréal Hires out bicycles and roller blades as well as offering riding tours of Vieux-Montréal and Vieux-Port.

🚇 G7 ✉ Quai King-Edward ☎ 847 0666 🕐 Apr–Oct: daily 9–9

WALKING TOURS

Guidatour Guided walks of Vieux-Montréal.

🚇 G7 ✉ 477 Saint-François-Xavier ☎ 844 4021 🚾 Place d'Armes

Phantômes Vieux-Montréal Evening walks in the old city encountering some of Montréal's most famous ghosts.

🚇 G6 ✉ rue Saint-Paul Est at rue Bonsecours ☎ 868 0303

SPECIALISED TOURS

Tours Maisonneuve Visits places associated with famous Montréalers, such as churches containing the splendid stained glass of Italian-born artist Guido Nincheri (1885–1973), or the haunts of popular pre-war singer La Bolduc, whose real name was Mary Travers.

🚇 H1 ✉ Marché Maisonneuve ☎ 256 4636 🚾 Pie-IX

Day Trips

Orléans Express (☎ 842 2281) and Gray Line (☎ 934 1222) offer excursions to Québec City, the hills of the Laurentians and the vineyards of the Eastern Townships. Particularly popular are autumn foliage tours and trips to the Roman Catholic shrine at Sainte-Anne-de-Beaupré just outside Québec City. Croisières Navimex (☎ 849 9136) offer voyages to Québec City.

A harbour-cruise ship

EXCURSIONS

MUSÉE FERROVIAIRE

If you have even a passing interest in trains and railways, visit the Musée Ferroviaire Canadien (Canadian Railway Museum), one of North America's largest collections of steam engines and railway-related memorabilia. On the 15-acre site and in two vast hangars are trams, boxcars, steam engines, guard's vans, dining cars, diesels, trolley-buses, snow ploughs – even horse-drawn sleighs. Among the engines and train carriages on show are CPR 5935, one of the largest locomotives ever built; BR 60010, which once pulled the *Flying Scotsman* in Britain; and the *Saskatchewan*, the private carriage used by Sir William Van Horne while supervising construction of the Canadian Pacific Railway. Trams and steam engines can usually be seen working on Sundays.

OKA AND HUDSON

English-speaking Hudson provides a charming riverside escape from the city. Its pretty streets are ideal for strolling, and you can browse among its antique shops or have tea in one of the sedate tea shops. On summer Saturdays the town plays host to Finnegan's Market (Main Street), the largest antiques and flea market in Québec. A 10-minute ferry ride across the Ottawa River takes you to the orchard-covered hills of Oka, a pretty village whose tranquillity was marred in 1990 by a summer-long deadlock between the army and Mohawk natives, who were angry at plans to build a golf course on one of their ancient

INFORMATION

Musée Ferroviaire
Distance 19km south
Journey time 20–30 minutes
- ✉ 122a rue Saint-Pierre, Saint-Constant
- ☎ 450/632 2410
- 🕐 May–Aug: daily 9–5; Sep–Oct: Sat, Sun
- 🚇 Longueuil and Angrignon, then bus

Oka and Hudson
Distance 21km west
Journey time 20–30 minutes
- ✉ Abbey: 1600 chemin d'Oka, Oka
- 🕐 Abbey Mon–Fri 9:30–11:30, 1–5; Sat 9–5. Finnegan's Market May–late Oct: Sat
- ☎ Abbey 450/479 8361. Finnegan's Market 450/458 4377
- 🚉 Gare Windsor to Hudson, then ferry to Oka

Québec City

Sign up for an organised trip (▶ 19) or use public transport (journey time 2–3 hours). Orléans Express ☎ 842 2281 runs hourly express buses (6AM–1AM) from the Terminus Voyageur bus station. VIA Rail ☎ 871 1331 runs four trains daily on weekdays and three on Saturdays and Sundays.

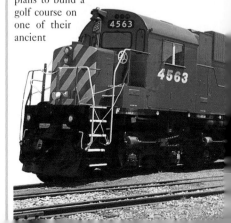

Locomotives at the Canadian Railway Museum

burial sites. Calm has returned, however, and so have the pilgrims who come here every year to make the Stations of the Cross at the Calvaire d'Oka, a commemoration of Christ's passion and death built by Sulpician priests in 1739. Another holy site is the Cistercian abbey founded by French monks in 1880. Its charming gardens and austerely beautiful church are open to all.

LACHINE

Lachine, on the southern edge of Montréal, makes an interesting little break from the city centre. The best-known of its sights is the Lieu historique national du Commerce-de-la-Fourrure (Fur Trade National Historic Site), a beautifully sited stone trading-post built for the Hudson's Bay Company in 1803. Today, displays highlight the history of the Canadian fur trade. Close by is the Centre d'Interprétation du Canal de Lachine, an interpretation centre devoted to the Lachine Canal, built to bypass some of the more treacherous stretches of the St Lawrence River. Lachine's Musée de la Ville, a museum of pioneer memorabilia, is housed in one of Montréal's oldest buildings, a former trading-post built in 1669. One way you might see this area is to hire a bike and cycle along the canal's towpath.

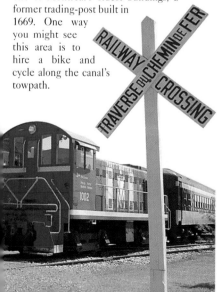

INFORMATION

Lachine
Distance 9.7km
Journey time 15 minutes
Historic Site
- ✉ 1255 boulevard Saint-Joseph, Lachine
- ☎ 637 7433
- ◷ Apr–mid-Oct: Mon 1–6; Tue–Sun 10–12:30, 1–6. Mid-Oct–early Dec: Wed–Sun 9:30–12:30, 1–5

Interpretation Centre
- ✉ Boulevard Saint-Joseph at 7ième Avenue
- ☎ 637 7433
- ◷ Mid-May–early Sep: Mon 1–6; Tue–Sun 10–noon, 1–6

Museum
- ✉ 110 chemin LaSalle (9.7km south of downtown)
- ☎ 634 3471
- ◷ Apr–mid-Dec: Wed–Sun 11:30–4:30
- ◐ Angrignon
- ▭ 195 Ouest for Historic Site and Interpretation Centre; 110 for Museum

Eastern Townships and the Laurentians

The Townships to the east and the Laurentians to the northwest are a short drive away. Their mountains and lakes make them ideal for hiking and swimming in summer or skiing and snow-mobiling in winter. There are vineyards, while antique shops and restaurants fill the villages.

WHAT'S ON

January/February　*Fête des Neiges*: Ice and snow celebrations on Îles Notre-Dame and Sainte-Hélène.

March　*St Patrick's Day Parade*: North America's third largest, plus informal blues sessions in rue Saint-Denis bars.

April–September　*Montréal Expos*: The city baseball team plays.

May　*Festival de Théâtre des Ameriques*: New drama.

June　*Festival du Nouveau Cinéma*: Independent and avant-garde films and video.
Benson and Hedges International Fireworks Competition: Pyrotechnics on Thursdays and Sundays mid-June to mid-July.
Grand Prix du Canada: Formula 1 racing on Île Notre-Dame.
Tour d'Île: As many as 40,000 cyclists of all ages participate in this non-competitive 66km trek through city streets.
Fête Vieux-Port: Concerts, dancing and other entertainment until the first Monday in September.
Mozart Plus: Montréal Symphony Orchestra concerts in Basilique Notre-Dame.

July　*International Jazz Festival:* Largest celebration of jazz music in the world with lots of free open-air concerts.
Juste Pour Rire (Just for Laughs): The world's largest comedy festival.
Nuits d'Afrique: Traditional African music and festivities on boulevard Saint-Laurent.
Franco Folies: More than 1,000 musicians participate in this celebration of French songs and music.

August　*Omnium du Maurier*: International tennis.
Les Fêtes Gourmandes Internationales de Montréal: Open-air festival where you can sample delicacies from around the world.
Festival des Films du Monde: World film festival.

September–May　*L'Opéra de Montréal*: The Montréal Opera season runs from mid-September to mid-May.

MONTRÉAL's
top 25 sights

The sights are shown on the maps on the inside front cover and inside back cover, numbered **1–25** *from west to east across the city*

BIODÔME DE MONTRÉAL

The Biôdome has been a success ever since it opened in 1992 in what used to be the Olympic cycle-racing stadium. This living museum integrates birds animals, and plants into superb re-creations of their natural habitats.

HIGHLIGHTS

- 'Waterbabies'
- Parrots
- Otters
- Lynx
- Penguins

INFORMATION

- ⊞ G1
- ✉ 4777 avenue Pierre-de-Coubertin
- ☎ 868 3000
- 🕐 Mid-Jun—early Sep: daily 9–7. Early Sep—mid-Jun: daily 9–5
- 🍴 Café
- 🚇 Viau
- ♿ Excellent
- 🎫 Expensive (joint ticket available with Jardin botanique and L'Insectarium)
- ↔ Parc olympique (▶ 25), Jardin botanique (▶ 26)
- ❓ Gift shop

Sea life enjoyed without having to get wet

Habitats   Montréal's Biodôme, the only one of its kind in the world, replicates four of the most beautiful habitats in North, Central and South America – tropical forest, the St Lawrence marine eco-system, Laurentian forest and the polar world – with their plants, birds, marine creatures and other animals. You watch otters frolicking in waterfalls, observe marine creatures through glass and peek at animals and preening birds through the foliage of living forest. But this is more than an indoor zoo. It is actively involved in breeding endangered species in captivity with the aim of one day releasing the offspring into the wild.

Animals   As you walk into the first habitat, the Amazonian rain forest, heat, humidity and primal smells hit you immediately. Exotic birds chirp overhead, while the leafy undergrowth is alive with crocodiles, capybaras (or 'water-baby', one of the world's largest rodents) and golden lion tamarins (orange-furred monkeys which are increasingly scarce in their native Brazil). You'll also see darting parrots, a cave full of bats (behind glass), and other mammals, amphibians, reptiles and fish. In the Laurentian forest you can watch lynx, otter, beaver and porcupine. A 2.5-million litre tank in the St Lawrence marine ecosystem re-creates a miniature sea complete with nesting gannets and a tidal pool filled with anemones and sea urchins. The most popular exhibits – the puffins and penguins – are in the polar exhibition.

Parc olympique

During the 1976 summer Olympic Games, a Romanian gymnast named Nadia Comaneci electrified the world with her perfect performances. But when the games ended, they left an architectural and financial legacy that still divides the city.

Cost When Mayor Jean Drapeau persuaded Montréalers to host the Olympic Games in 1976 he promised that the likelihood of the event costing them a cent would be about the same as that of a man having a baby. French architect Roger Taillibert set to work believing money was no object. Both were wrong. The stadium and its famous tower cost $1.2 billion, and Québec smokers are still paying off the debt with a special tax on tobacco. Locals now call the stadium the 'Big O', partly in reference to its circular shape, and partly as a result of the huge amount of money still 'owed' on the project. The stadium itself has never been much of a success as a sports venue, abandoned by the local football team, with the Expos, Montréal's major-league baseball team, also trying to leave. The place makes its money from trade shows and huge concerts. But it's impressively bright and airy, and worth seeing.

Leaning tower It is not so much the stadium that pulls in visitors, however, but the park's famous inclined tower (Tour de Montréal), built to support the stadium's retractable roof. Since it opened in 1989, over 3 million people have ascended the 175m to the observation platform. The ascent via an external cable car is stomach-churning, but you are rewarded with a mesmerising view that on clear days stretches for some 80km. Galleries in the tower's lower levels contain displays about the park's history and the Tourist Hall at the tower's base has information, tickets and exhibits.

DID YOU KNOW?

- Cost: $1.2 billion
- Completed: 1989
- Years late: 13
- Usage: 250 days a year (world's highest stadium usage)
- Seats: 55,147
- Area: 6ha
- Area: space for seven jumbo jets
- World's tallest inclined tower
- Lean: 23–45 degrees
- Leaning Tower of Pisa: 5 degrees
- Weight of cables: 190 tonnes
- Cable-car: 270m in two minutes

INFORMATION

- G1
- 4141 avenue Pierre-de-Coubertin
- 252 8687
- 12 Jun–early Sep: Mon noon–9; Tue–Sun 10–9. Mid-Sep–9 Jan, 12 Feb–early Jun and hols: Mon noon–5; Tue–Sun 11–5. Guided tours in French daily 11 and 2; in English 12:40 and 3:40
- Cafés
- Viau
- 185
- Very good
- Biodôme de Montréal (➤ 24), Jardin botanique (➤ 26)
- Souvenir shop

JARDIN BOTANIQUE DE MONTRÉAL

DID YOU KNOW?

- Area: 75ha
- Flora: 26,000 species
- Specimens: 36,000
- Bonsai: largest collection in North America
- Chinese Garden: largest outside Asia
- Insects in L'Insectarium: 149,000; on display 20,000
- Muscles in house fly: 5,000

INFORMATION

- ⊞ G1
- ✉ Jardin botanique 4101 rue Sherbrooke Est; Insectarium 4581 rue Sherbrooke Est
- ☎ Jardin botanique 872 1400; Insectarium 868 3056
- ◷ Late Jun–early Sep: daily 9–8. Mid-Sep–mid-Jun: daily 9–6
- 🍴 Café
- Ⓥ Viau, Pie IX
- ⓰ Very good
- 🎟 Moderate (reduced rates off-season; combined ticket available with Biodôme)
- ⇄ Biodôme de Montréal (➤ 24), Parc olympique (➤ 25)
- 🚌 Free shuttle bus from Le Biodôme and Viau Métro. Japanese tea ceremony enacted in entrance pavilion; phone for times

Montréal has the world's second largest botanical gardens – no small feat given the cruel climate. They are a glorious blend of exotic horticultural excess, with hundreds of beautiful flowers, combined with the tranquillity of a formal garden.

Gardens Montréal's lovely botanical gardens are the second largest in the world after Kew Gardens in London. Opened in 1931, they now comprise some 30 different outdoor gardens and 10 vast exhibition greenhouses. Each garden represents a different climate, country or style, ranging from a collection of poisonous plants to gardens devoted to orchids or medicinal herbs. Nearby lies the Insectarium, in a suitably insect-shaped building. Its galleries are filled with all manner of displays and countless insects living and dead (and exotic butterflies in summer). Don't miss the gargantuan South American cockroaches. In February, visitors can try some truly high-protein morsels as local cooks whip up chocolate-covered ants, honey-dipped bees and the ever popular insect-centred lollipops.

Shanghai surprise The gardens' highlight is the 1991 2ha Montréal-Shanghai Dream Lake Garden, a perfect replica of one from the Ming dynasty (1368–1644), and designed to celebrate the friendship between the two cities. Lakes, rocks and plants strive for a harmonious blend of *yin* and *yang*: small and large, soft and hard, light and dark, flowing and immovable. Look for the seven elegant pavilions, central reflecting pool, large rockery and collection of miniature trees known as 'penjings' (on display in summer only). Also exquisite is the Japanese Garden and Pavilion, home to a minimalist mineral Zen garden, as well as a summer collection of Japanese bonsai trees.

The Montréal-Shanghai Dream Lake Garden

PARC DU MONT-ROYAL

Mont-Royal is only 233m above sea level – a mere geological pimple – but Montréalers call it, without irony, 'the Mountain', an appropriately grand appellation given the hold this steep, green oasis has on their affections.

History   Mont-Royal is one of seven such peaks on the St Lawrence plain, all composed of intrusive rock hard enough to have survived the glacial scraping of the last Ice Age. Explorer Jacques Cartier named the hill – probably in honour of his royal patron, Francis I of France – on his first voyage up the St Lawrence in 1535 (► 12). The area became a park in 1877, following the local council's fear (after a particularly severe winter) that the forested slopes were being denuded by Montréalers' quest for firewood. The land was bought for $1 million, and landscaped by designer Frederick Law Olmsted, who was also responsible for New York's Central Park and San Francisco's Golden Gate Park.

Attractions   The park is too large to see in a day, so choose a corner to explore. A bike gives more opportunities for seeing farther afield. Most people on foot enter at the Monument Sir-George-Étienne-Cartier, a popular summer venue for street musicians, vendors and people-watchers. Olmsted Road leads to the famous Montréal Cross (1924) on the summit. Beaver Lake, created in the 1930s, is another focal point, as is Le Chalet, which has fantastic views and an interpretation centre. Calixa Lavallée, composer of Canada's national anthem, is buried in the Roman Catholic Cimetière Notre-Dame-des-Neiges, one of two huge cemeteries situated on the park's northern perimeter, and Ann Leonowens, immortalised in *The King and I*, is in the Protestant Mont-Royal Cemetery.

HIGHLIGHTS

- Montréal Cross
- Le Chalet viewpoint
- Beaver Lake
- Notre-Dame-des-Neiges Cemetery
- Mont-Royal Cemetery

INFORMATION

- B8–E6
- Monument Sir-George-Étienne-Cartier and other entrances
- 844 4928
- Daily 6AM–midnight
- The Chalet
- Mont-Royal
- 11, 66, 80, 107, 129, 144, 165
- Some steep paths
- Free
- Oratoire Saint-Joseph (► 28), Musée des beaux-arts (► 31), McCord Museum (► 30)

DID YOU KNOW?

- Area: 202.5ha
- Paths: 56km
- Ski-paths: 19km
- Bodies in cemeteries: 1 million plus
- Paths in cemeteries: 55km
- Height of Montréal Cross: 30m
- Distance Cross is visible when lit: over 88km

Mont-Royal view

5

ORATOIRE SAINT-JOSEPH

The huge dome of the Oratoire Saint-Joseph, one of the world's largest, is a distinctive landmark on the Montréal skyline, and the huge church beneath it is the most important Roman Catholic shrine dedicated to Christ's earthly father.

Miracle cures   The story of the Oratoire Saint-Joseph begins with Brother André Bessette, a diminutive, barely literate man born in 1837 to a poor rural family. He joined a religious order – the Congrégation du Saint-Croix – and worked as a porter in the order's classical college at the foot of Mont-Royal. He built a small shrine to his favourite saint on the mountain slopes and cared for sick pilgrims. He developed an extraordinary reputation as a healer, and donations began to pour into his order from grateful pilgrims who wanted to help André fulfil his dream of building a grand monument to St Joseph. Construction began in 1924 and Brother André lived long enough to see the completion of the crypt church, but the main church with its dome was not finished until 1937, long after his death.

Interior   André was beatified in 1982 and buried in the oratory, which also includes part of his original chapel, a small museum about his life, the room in which he died (removed wholesale from a local hospice) and, in a jar on the high altar, his preserved heart (occasionally said to quiver miraculously). Also here is a 56-bell carillon originally cast for the Eiffel Tower but never installed; the bells were loaned to the oratory in 1955 and later bought. There are free carillon and organ recitals all year round. Be sure to climb to the observatory, one of Montréal's highest points, for a superb view, and to study the fine Carrera marble sculptures marking the Stations of the Cross outside in Mont-Royal.

The oratory's vast dome

DID YOU KNOW?

- Height: 260m
- Seating capacity: 3,003 (standing 10,000)
- Christmas cribs: over 30
- From: 103 countries
- Bells in carillon: 56

INFORMATION

- ✚ B8
- ✉ 3800 chemin Queen Mary near Côtes-des-Neiges
- ☎ 733 8211
- ◷ Daily 9–5
- 🍴 Cafeteria
- Ⓜ Côte-des-Neiges
- 🚌 51, 144, 165, 166, 535 (peak hours)
- ♿ Very good
- 📷 Oratory free. Museum donation
- 🔗 Parc du Mont-Royal (➤ 27)

6

McGill University

On a cold night, if you stand on the stone steps along the southern wall of McGill's glass-and-concrete Leacock Building when the snow is falling thick and fast, and look out across the whitened campus at the glittering city towers, you could fall in love with winter.

Urban country The university opened in 1821, far from the city limits on Mont-Royal's lower slopes, on a patch of pasture donated for the purpose by fur-trader and land-speculator James McGill. Since then, Montréal has spread inexorably northwards and now surrounds the 32ha campus. McGill offers not so much a respite from the busy city as a privileged place from which to view it and feel its vibrant rhythms.

Architecture The Greek Revival Roddick Gates guard the main entrance to the university on rue Sherbrooke Ouest, and behind them a long tree-lined avenue leads to the 1839 neoclassical domed Arts Building, the oldest of the 70 or so buildings on campus. Inside is Moyse Hall, a lovely theatre dating from 1926. Along the avenue's east side are two fine neoclassical buildings designed in the 1890s by Sir Andrew Taylor, who also designed the Library with its elaborately carved columns and gargoyles. Percy Nobbs's 1908 Macdonald Engineering Building is a remarkable example of the English Baroque Revival style. But the most beautiful structure on campus is the temple-like Redpath Museum of Natural History, which is one of the country's oldest museums, housing a huge and wonderfully whimsical collection that includes dinosaur bones, old coins, African art and a shrunken head. On the lawn outside is a fine stone fountain, and under the trees a bronze statue of James McGill hurries across campus holding his tricorn hat against the wind.

HIGHLIGHTS

- Roddick Gates
- Green space
- Redpath Museum
- Views
- Arts Building

INFORMATION

- E7
- 805 rue Sherbrooke Ouest
- Redpath Museum
  398 4086
- Sep–May: Mon–Fri 9–5; Sun 1–5. Jun–Aug: Mon–Thu 9–5; Sun 1–5
- McGill
- Fair
- Free
- Parc du Mont-Royal (► 27), McCord Museum (► 30), Musée des beaux-arts (► 31), Christ Church Cathedral (► 33)

Outside the Macdonald Engineering Building

McCord Museum

INFORMATION

➕ E7

✉ 690 rue Sherbrooke Ouest at rue Victoria

☎ 398 7100

🕐 Mon and hols 10–6; Tue–Fri 10–6; Sat, Sun 10–5.

🍴 The McCord Café

Ⓜ McGill

🚌 24, 125

♿ Good

💲 Moderate (free Sat 10–noon)

↔ McGill University (➤ 29), Musée des beaux-arts (➤ 31), Christ Church Cathedral (➤ 33), Musée d'art contemporain (➤ 36)

❓ Guided tours, reading room

One of Canada's best history museums, the McCord Museum of Canadian History possesses a huge breadth of artefacts, including an important photographic collection, which provide a fascinating insight into Montréal's past.

Museum Montréal lawyer David Ross McCord (1844–1930), the scion of a prosperous Scots-Irish family, was a collector with an insatiable appetite for anything with Canadian history. In the 1920s he gave his huge collection of books, furniture, clothing, guns, paintings, documents, toys and photographs to McGill University, where it was housed in the McGill Union Building (1906). A $20-million renovation in 1992 doubled the museum's size, but still there is space to display only a fragment of its 90,000-piece collection.

A Native Canadian totem pole

Photographs The museum is strongest on the art, culture and history of Native Canadians, or First Peoples, and devotes several intriguing galleries to native furs, carvings and embroidered beadwork. The collections also include some 10,000 costumes, many dating from the 18th century and earlier. One of the museum's most remarkable possessions is the Notman Archives, a collection of prints and glass prints produced by photographic pioneer William Notman, who captured Victorian life in Montréal. They include photographs of formal balls, soldiers marching and members of the exclusive Montréal Athletic Association in snowshoes. Each of the hundreds of people shown in these pictures was photographed individually in the studio and then painstakingly mounted on the appropriate background.

MUSÉE DES BEAUX-ARTS

Canada's oldest art museum (founded in 1860) consists of the Museum of Fine Arts and its magnificent new Desmarais Pavilion, and has the best collection of Canadian paintings in the country, as well as Native Canadian artefacts and many fine Old Masters.

Museum Radical alterations have made this venerable institution one of North America's finest galleries. Completed in 1912 and enlarged in 1976, the main building is an unmistakable feature of rue Sherbrooke, with its stolid Vermont marble front and four enormous Ionic columns. Across the street stands the Desmarais Pavilion (1991), a stunning modern building designed by well-known Montréal architect Moshe Safdie. Wonderful views across the city open up from its upper levels, and underground galleries connect it with the original building.

Collection Canadian paintings range from works imported by the earliest French settlers through to those by artists from the Toronto-based Group of Seven. Note the fine landscapes, and the paintings by the so-called Automatistes, who dominated Montréal's art world during the 1940s. Many Native Canadian artefacts are on display, along with period furnishings, drawings, engravings, silverware and art from ancient China, Japan, Egypt, Greece and South America. Among the Old Masters originally bought by wealthy Montréal fur traders are those by El Greco, Rembrandt, and Memlinc; more recent eras are represented by Picasso, Henry Moore and the Impressionists. The Museum of Decorative Arts (Musée des arts décoratifs ► 50), across the covered Passage Culturel behind the Desmarais Pavilion, has a superb collection of ceramics, fabrics and furniture.

HIGHLIGHTS

- *Portrait of a Young Woman*, Rembrandt
- *Portrait of a Man*, El Greco
- *Torso*, Henry Moore
- *October*, James Tissot

James Tissot's October

INFORMATION

- ✚ E8
- ✉ 1379–80 rue Sherbrooke Ouest
- ☎ 285 1600
- 🕐 Tue, Thu–Sun 11–6; Wed 11–9
- 🍴 Café du Musée, Le Mitoyen restaurant
- Ⓖ Guy-Concordia
- 🚌 24
- ♿ Good
- ⓘ Free permanent exhibition free. Special shows expensive

31

9

CANADIAN CENTRE FOR ARCHITECTURE

HIGHLIGHTS

- Façade
- Halls
- Mansion
- Conservatory
- Gardens

INFORMATION

- E8
- 1920 rue Baile between rues St-Marc and du Fort
- 939 7026
- Jun–Sep: Tue, Wed, Fri–Sun 11–6; Thu 11–8. Oct–May: Wed, Fri 11–6; Thu 11–8; Sat, Sun 11–5
- Guy-Concordia, Atwater
- 15, 150, 535
- Excellent
- Centre moderate (free Thu 6–8). Sculpture Gardens free
- Musée des beaux-arts (➤ 31)
- Guided tours of building and gardens Sun 2:30 (French), 3:30 (English)

DID YOU KNOW?

- Books: 180,000
- Photographs: 50,000
- Prints and drawings: 65,000
- Periodicals: 700

There's something fitting about the layout of what is arguably the world's premier architectural museum. Its silvery U-shaped fortress embraces an impressive 19th-century mansion built for one of Montreal's great plutocrats.

Temple of architecture The grey limestone façade is not terribly welcoming. Long and low, it is virtually windowless, and the front door, at the building's western end, appears to be an afterthought. But that door leads into six beautifully lit halls given over to changing exhibits ranging from the academic to the whimsical – displays on modernist theory and American lawn culture are equally at home. Incorporated into the complex is the 1877 Shaughnessy Mansion, with its striking art nouveau conservatory, built for the chairman of the Canadian Pacific Railway Sir Thomas Shaughnessy. Across the road, in a little island of green between two main streets, is a garden designed by Melvin Charney, where fanciful fragments – a set of Doric columns here, a Victorian doorway there – tell the story of architecture.

History The woman behind all this is architect Phyllis Lambert. A fierce defender of Montreal's architectural heritage, she founded the centre in 1979 and presided, with architect Peter Rose, over the building of its present home (1985–9). She also contributed her own impressive collection to the centre – 65,000 prints and drawings (some by Michelangelo and Leonardo da Vinci), 50,000 architectural photographs and 180,000 books and publications dating from 15th-century manuscripts to the present. The collection forms the backbone of the centre's archives, which are open by appointment.

CHRIST CHURCH CATHEDRAL

The seat of Montréal's Anglican bishop is a graceful ship of serenity floating (almost literally) on a sea of commerce. Not only are there department stores on either side of it and a skyscraper behind, but there is a popular shopping mall right underneath.

Copy This beautifully simple church is the city's Anglican cathedral, built between 1857 and 1859 at the instigation of Francis Fulford, Montréal's first Anglican bishop. Its neo-Gothic style is reminiscent of a 14th-century English church, but its plan is actually an exact copy of the Anglican cathedral in Fredericton, New Brunswick, which was designed by the same architect Frank Wills. It was originally faced with stone imported from Caën in Normandy, but was replaced with Indiana limestone. The steeple had problems, too. It was too heavy for the soft, unstable ground and was replaced in 1927 with one made of aluminium plates, craftily doctored to match the stone of the rest of the church. Among the notable artefacts inside the church is a cross made from nails rescued from Coventry Cathedral, which was bombed in 1940.

Money matters Over time, soaring towers have dwarfed the cathedral, while high maintenance costs and dwindling congregations led to a budgetary shortfall. The Anglican authorities found an imaginative solution in 1985 when they leased the land around and beneath the cathedral to developers. Ground under the building was removed, leaving the church supported by metal girders and balanced precariously above a yawning chasm; the church now sits on top of Les Promenades de la Cathédrale, a busy mall. Shoppers, office workers and shop clerks of all faiths retreat to the cathedral at midday for free concerts and organ recitals.

Top: the world beneath the cathedral
Above: the cathedral, dwarfed by skyscrapers

INFORMATION

➕ F7

✉ 635 rue Sainte-Catherine Ouest and avenue Union

☎ Recorded information 288 6421. Cathedral staff 843 6577

🕐 Daily 8–6

Ⓜ McGill

♿ Very good; long ramps from street

🍽 Free

🔁 McGill University (➤ 29), McCord Museum (➤ 30), Musée des beaux-arts (➤ 31), Cathédrale Marie-Reine-du-Monde (➤ 35), Musée d'art contemporain (➤ 36)

❓ Noon and evening choral and organ concerts

UNDERGROUND CITY

HIGHLIGHTS

- Rubber-tyred Métro
- Shopping
- Opera (Place des Arts)
- Hockey (Molson Centre)
- Baseball (Olympic Stadium)
- Indoor Skating (1000 de la Gauchetière)

INFORMATION

- E7–F8
- Access at métro stations in city centre
- Sun–Fri 5:30AM–12:30AM; Sat 5:30AM–1AM
- Peel, McGill, Bonaventure, Place-des-Arts, Square-Victoria
- Fair

It's possible to arrive in Montréal by train in mid-January and spend a pleasant week without once stepping outside. You could shop, dine, see an opera, watch a hockey game, go to church or even attend a university lecture without putting on your coat.

Beginnings Montréal's vast underground city began modestly enough in the early 1960s, when a mall full of shops and boutiques opened underneath the main plaza of Place Ville-Marie, the city's first modern skyscraper. Both it and the neighbouring Queen Elizabeth Hotel were built over the Canadian National Railway's tracks so it seemed natural enough to link both of them with Central Station, and to Place Bonaventure to the south. The idea caught on, not surprisingly in a city with bitter winters and humid summers, and really took off when the Métro opened in 1966.

Growth The Underground now has 29km of wide, well-lit tunnels, mostly clustered around 10 of the 64km-long Métro system's 65 stations. At the last count, the system encompassed seven major hotels, two universities, both train stations, more than 1,600 boutiques, two department stores, more than 200 restaurants, at least 30 cinemas, the Olympic Stadium, and the Molson Centre. The only universities are French – the Université de Montréal and the Université du Québec à Montréal (UQAM). Oddly enough in a city that was once so Roman Catholic, the only church with its own link to the system is the Protestant Christ Church Cathedral. Remember that only the links are underground; most of the shops and malls are above ground. In fact, the soaring glass foyer of Place des Arts is as much a part of the system as the deepest Métro station.

Top: inside the Desjardins complex

Above: Métro entrance

CATHÉDRALE MARIE-REINE-DU-MONDE

Mary Queen of the World Cathedral brings the Italian Renaissance into the heart of Montréal. Dwarfed now by skyscrapers, the cathedral was a deliberate and daring monument to 19th-century Roman Catholic triumphalism when it was first built.

Looking up into the dome of the cathedral

Imitation Bishop Ignace Bourget, who began the cathedral two years after Canadian confederation, intended to underline papal supremacy and remind the world that Catholicism still dominated what was then the largest city in the new Dominion. So he set the cathedral at the heart of the city's Anglo-Protestant district, and designed it as a one-quarter-sized replica of St Peter's in Rome. Begun in 1870, the building was completed in 1894. The figures outside, often mistaken for the Apostles, represent the patron saints of parishes in the Archdiocese of Montréal.

Interior In contrast to the lovely intimacy of Notre-Dame in Vieux-Montréal, the interior is sombre, although the interiors of both churches are the work of architect Victor Bourgeau. The gloom was intended to intensify the effect of candles and accentuate the rose windows. The opulent high altar features a copy of the vast baldacchino, or altar canopy, by Bernini in St Peter's, while the first little chapel in the left aisle has a red-flocked sanctuary filled with medals and saintly relics. Bishop Bourget is interred in a second chapel on the same side of the church, his recumbent figure surrounded by the tombs of his successors. One last sign of Montréal's loyalty to the Holy See is mounted on a pillar facing the bishop's tomb – a memorial to the men from the diocese who served in the Papal Zouaves in the fight against Italian nationalists.

HIGHLIGHTS

- Stained glass
- High altar
- Bourget chapel

INFORMATION

- F8
- 1085 rue de la Cathédrale
- 866 1661
- Daily 7–7
- Bonaventure
- 38, 107, 150, 410, 420, 535
- Very good: steep ramp
- Free
- Christ Church Cathedral (► 33), St Patrick's Basilica (► 37)

35

13

MUSÉE D'ART CONTEMPORAIN

HIGHLIGHTS

- Architecture
- *Lips*, Geneviève Cadieux
- Steel atrium
- Sculpture garden
- *L'Île fortifiée*, Paul-Émile Borduas

INFORMATION

- ✚ F7
- ✉ 185 rue Sainte-Catherine Ouest at rue Jeanne-Mance
- ☎ 847 6226
- 🕐 Tue, Thu–Sun 11–6; Wed 11–9
- 🍴 La Rotonde restaurant (lunch and dinner)
- Ⓜ Place-des-Arts
- 🚌 14, 15, 80, 129, 535 (peak hours)
- ♿ Excellent
- 💷 Moderate; free Wed from 6PM for collection, half-rate for exhibitions; some free weekend programmes
- ↔ McCord Museum (► 30), Christ Church Cathedral (► 33), St Patrick's Basilica (► 37)
- ❓ Guided tours, weekend programmes and child activities

A pair of billboard-sized lips – illuminated at night – marks Canada's only major museum of contemporary art. Its building is as impressive as the collection it houses, from its offbeat doors to the distinctive angular galleries and central atrium.

Building Founded in 1964 by the Québec government, the museum occupied three different buildings before moving into its present home, a superb plain-faced modern building only a stone's throw from the Place des Arts (► 81), in 1992. It originally focused on the work of indigenous Québécois artists, but the museum has increasingly widened its scope and now mounts temporary exhibitions of work by artists from all around the world. It has hosted well over 600 exhibitions, and attracted some 1.6 million visitors.

Paintings Works of art in the gallery date from around 1939 up to the present day with at least 60 per cent of the more than 5,000 works of art in the museum's collection being from Québécois artists. Among those represented are David Moore, Alfred Pellan, Jean-Paul Riopelle, with 75 paintings by Montréal artist Paul-Émile Borduas on display; Canadian artists include Jack Bush, Michael Snow and Barbara Steinman; works by Picasso, Lichtenstein and Warhol are also on view. There is a growing video art collection, started in 1979. Much of the permanent collection is often moved out to make way for temporary exhibitions, such as retrospectives of the work of Guido Molinari, one of Canada's leading abstract artists, and Henry Saxe, one of the country's foremost sculptors, and exhibitions of recent acquisitions. Remember to look around the impressive sculpture garden, which includes work by Pierre Granche.

St Patrick's Basilica

Every day visitors arrive by the busload to soak up the glories of the Basilique Notre-Dame-de-Montréal. Just a few blocks north, the pious and the knowledgeable have the delicate gold and green beauty of St Patrick's Basilica to themselves.

History Bishop Ignace Bourget gave only grudging approval when the Irish Catholics of his diocese asked for a church of their own in 1843. The mass, he reasoned, was in Latin, and most of the Irish spoke Gaelic at home, not English. Surely they could go to church with their French-speaking brethren. But the Irish persisted and with help from the Sulpician priests erected one of Canada's most graceful neo-Gothic churches.

Features On sunny afternoons, light floods through the stained-glass figures of the four evangelists, and colours the soaring nave with a honey-coloured glow. The ceiling over the sanctuary gleams with green and gold mosaics and the air smells of a mixture of beeswax polish and incense. The pulpit is decorated with panels of the 12 apostles, a huge sanctuary lamp is graced with half a dozen six-foot angels, and poet Emile Nelligan was baptised in the ornate font. But what sets the church apart is the overwhelming presence of the communion of saints. Dozens of statues of bishops, martyrs, missionaries, princesses and peasants jostle for space on the main altar and crowd the niches of the side altars. Another 150 holy men and women are honoured in painted panels that line the walls of the nave. And at least one of the fathers of the confederation of Canada is remembered as well. Parishioner Thomas Darcy McGee was buried from St Patrick's after his assassination in 1868. His pew (No. 240) is towards the back, marked with a Canadian flag.

HIGHLIGHTS

- Pulpit
- Sanctuary lamp
- Baptismal font
- Saints
- Darcy McGee's pew

INFORMATION

- ✚ F7
- ✉ 460 boulevard René-Lévesque Ouest
- ☎ 866 7379
- ◷ Daily 9–6
- Ⓜ McGill
- ♿ Fair
- ⓘ Free
- ↔ Christ Church Cathedral (► 33), Cathédrale Marie-Reine-du-Monde (► 35), Basilique Notre-Dame (► 38)

Top and above: the saintly embellishments of the main altar

37

15

BASILIQUE NOTRE-DAME

HIGHLIGHTS

- Pulpit
- Wood carving
- Stained glass
- High altar

INFORMATION

- ✚ G7
- ✉ 110 rue Notre-Dame Ouest
- ☎ Basilica 842 2925
- 🕐 Late Jun–early Sep: daily 7AM–8PM. Early Sep–late Jun: daily 7–6
- Ⓜ Place-d'Armes
- 🚌 38, 55, 129
- ♿ Very good: one step into church
- 💰 Moderate. Free if you are there to pray
- ↔ St Patrick's Basilica (➤ 37), Centre d'histoire de Montréal (➤ 39), Pointe-à-Callière (➤ 40), Vieux-Port de Montréal (➤ 45)
- ❓ Guided tours mid-May–late Jun, early Sep–mid-Oct: daily 9–4:30 every half-hour

DID YOU KNOW?

- Seats: 3,500
- Standing: 2,000
- Weight of bell: 11,240kg
- Bell-ringers once required: 12
- Organ pipes: 7,000

No other site in Montréal sums up the city's religious heritage as beautifully as the Basilica of Notre-Dame, a church whose seductive interior – Romanesque with touches of rococo – transports you into a world of almost perfect calm.

History Founded in 1627, Notre-Dame is on the flanks of the Place d'Armes, long the historic focus of the old city. The original church was replaced by the present neo-Gothic basilica between 1824 and 1829, and it was the largest religious edifice in North America when it was inaugurated. Today there is a brutish sky-scraper on the square's western side, but the church's twin towers – nicknamed Temperance and Perseverance – still command the skyline. The western tower, built in 1843, contains the famous 'Gros Bourdon', an 11,240kg bell whose peal can be heard up to 25km away.

Highly decorated Inside, thousands of tiny 24-carat gold stars stud the dusky blue, vaulted ceiling, and 14 stained-glass windows, brought from Limoges in 1929, tell the story of Ville-Marie's early development. But most of the interior is a tribute to the wood-working skills of Québec artists and artisans. All the figures in the life-sized tableaux behind the main altar are carved in wood as is the spectacular pulpit with its curving staircase on the east side of the nave. A fire in 1978 destroyed much of the large chapel behind the main altar. The Sulpician priests who run the church saved what they could of the original ornate woodwork and erected an enormous, modern bronze sculpture behind the altar. The chapel is still the most popular for weddings in Montréal; in 1994 pop diva Céline Dion married her manager in a ceremony that rivalled the pomp of a royal wedding.

CENTRE D'HISTOIRE DE MONTRÉAL

Although this history museum seems a little dated at first glance, in fact it tells Montréal's story in a charming way, allowing you to step in and share snippets of Montréalers' day-to-day lives from 1642 to the present.

History Of the monuments and historic sites that line Place d'Youville, one of Montréal's earliest market squares, the most attractive is the beautifully restored red stone Caserne Centrale de Pompiers, or old Central Fire Station (1903). Today this building houses the Centre d'histoire de Montréal, an 11-room interpretation centre which uses dioramas, videos and other devices to trace the city's development from Iroquois settlement to modern-day metropolis. Look for the mock-ups of the streetcar, the 19th-century factory and the gaudy 1940s living room. Temporary exhibitions on offbeat aspects of the city's history can often be found upstairs.

Also on the square On the south side of the Place d'Youville stand the Youville Stables (Écuries d'Youville), grey stone buildings constructed in 1828 as warehouses for grain merchants and soap manufacturers (the stables were next door). In 1967 the complex was converted into an attractive mixture of offices, shops and artisans' studios. Near the courtyard is Gibby's (►68), one of the city's best steak and seafood restaurants. Just off the square a plaque commemorates the Hôpital Général des Sœurs Grises (Grey Nuns' General Hospital), founded in 1694 as the city's second hospital and taken over in 1747 by Marguerite d'Youville, the wealthy widow who founded the Sœurs Grises. The order treated Montréal's sick, poor and elderly and established one of North America's first foundling hospitals.

HIGHLIGHTS

- Fire Station building
- Tram car
- Youville stables

INFORMATION

- ✚ G7
- ✉ 335, place d'Youville
- ☎ 872 3207
- 🕐 May–early Sep: daily 10–5. Early Sep–early Dec, mid-Jan–Apr: Tue–Sun 10–5
- Ⓜ Square-Victoria
- 🚌 38, 55, 61
- ♿ Moderate
- ✛ Basilique Notre-Dame (►38), Pointe-à-Callière (►40), Vieux-Port de Montréal (►45)
- ❓ Guided tours need to be arranged in advance

Below: tracing the city's development in the Centre d'histoire

17

POINTE-À-CALLIÈRE

The Musée d'archéologie et d'histoire de Montréal

Of all the innovations in the Vieux-Port, the superb Musée d'archéologie et d'histoire de Montréal at Pointe-à-Callière is the most impressive. It is the high point of developments that have given a little more heart and soul to old Montréal.

Archaeology and history Visit this magnificent modern museum on your first morning in Montréal: not only does it provide a fascinating introduction to the city's history, but it is also built at Pointe-à-Callière – the city's birthplace, the spot where Montréal's first 53 settlers landed from France on 17 May 1642. The museum uses high-tech audio-visual displays to tell the story of Montréal's development as a trading and meeting place.

Underground The main building of this $27-million museum is the stark, ship-like Édifice de l'Eperon, built on the foundations of the Royal Insurance building. It houses offices, temporary exhibits, a café with wonderful river views and a theatre with a 16-minute multi-media show on Montréal's history. But its real treasures are underground. The museum gives you access to the excavations underneath, where archaeologists have burrowed into the silt and rock to expose the layers of history. They have uncovered the remnants of a 19th-century sewer system, 18th-century tavern foundations and a cemetery dating to 1643. As you explore, you have virtual encounters with some of the city's more colourful citizens. Tunnels connect the excavations to the neoclassical Old Customs House, where there are still more exhibits and an extensive gift shop. The museum incorporates the Company 4 Pumphouse, which was the city's first electrical water-pumping system; it is now an exhibit on industrial development.

CHÂTEAU RAMEZAY

French governors, British conquerors and American generals have all stayed in this relic of the French regime. With its squat round towers and its rough stone finish, the Château Ramezay is like a bit of Normandy in North America.

History One of North America's most venerable buildings, this Norman-style country house was commissioned in 1705 by Claude de Ramezay, 11th governor of Montréal, and was the work of master-mason Pierre Couturier, one of the leading architects of his day (the distinctive round tower was a 19th-century addition). In 1745 de Ramezay's heir sold the property to governors of the Compagnie des Indes (West Indies Company), a fur-trading company that enjoyed a monopoly on all beaver pelts sold in French North America until the coming of the British. Under the French the house became the city's most fashionable meeting-place.

Museum After 1763 the building became home to the Governors General of British North America (1764–1849), and during the brief American invasion of 1775 served as a military headquarters for American commanders Benedict Arnold and Richard Montgomery. Benjamin Franklin was here later the same year, engaged in a doomed attempt to persuade Montréalers to join the United States. In 1895 the house was bought and turned into a museum, its interior fitted and furnished as it might have been in the 18th century with appropriate paintings, costumes and furniture; the kitchen, one of the most appealing parts of the house, is filled with period utensils, and the intricate carving of the wood-panelled Grande Salle is a graphic illustration of the opulence of 18th-century Montréal.

HIGHLIGHTS

- Grande Salle
- Portraits
- Kitchen

INFORMATION

- ✚ G6
- ✉ 280 rue Notre-Dame Est at rue Saint-Claude
- ☎ 861 3708
- 🕐 Jun–Sep: daily 10–6. Oct–May: Tue–Sun 10–4:30
- Ⓜ Champ-de-Mars
- 🚌 38
- ♿ Poor: ramp can be arranged, so visitors using wheelchairs should phone in advance
- 🍴 Moderate
- ↔ Lieu historique national Sir-G-E-Cartier (▶ 42), Chapelle Notre-Dame-de-Bonsecours (▶ 43), Vieux-Port (▶ 45)
- ❓ Chamber concerts: last Sun of month at 1:30, 2:30, 3:30. Gift shop

19

LIEU HISTORIQUE SIR G-E CARTIER

HIGHLIGHTS

- Commentaries
- Sound effects
- Life-sized models
- Canopied bed

INFORMATION

- ➕ G6
- ✉ 458 rue Notre-Dame Est at the corner of rue Berri
- ☎ 283 2282
- 🕐 Mid-Jun–Aug: daily 10–6. Early Apr–mid-June, Sep–Dec: Wed–Sun 10–noon, 1–5
- ➕ Champ-de-Mars
- 🚌 38
- ♿ Excellent, though visitors using wheelchairs should call one day in advance
- 💵 Inexpensive
- ↔ Château Ramezay (➤ 41), Chapelle Notre-Dame-de-Bonsecours (➤ 43), Marché Bonsecours (➤ 44), Vieux-Port de Montréal (➤ 45)
- ❓ Guided tours

With great charm, myriad original furnishings and artefacts beautifully re-create the ambience of domestic life in mid-19th-century Montréal in the former home of Sir George-Étienne Cartier (1814–73).

Cartier Sir George-Etienne Cartier, one of the founding fathers of Canadian confederation, was largely responsible for persuading French Canada to join the fledgling nation in 1867. In his youth, Cartier had thrown his support behind the abortive 1837 rebellion against British rule, but later became convinced that the new Canadian federation would give French Canadians the tools they needed to safeguard their religion, language and culture.

Museum The museum consists of two connected houses, both of which were home to the Cartier family between 1848 and 1872. The western half is concerned with Cartier's political and industrial preoccupations. He successfully promoted the construction of the Grand Trunk Railway; he worked on the abolition of Québec's seigneurial system (a hangover from the French regime) and the rewriting of its civil code; and he was Canada's first minister of defence. In one exhibit, you can sit in at a negotiating session with Cartier and the other Fathers of Confederation. The house on the east side of the museum uses ornate period furnishings to re-create the bourgeois life of the Cartier family in 19th-century Montréal. You can also eavesdrop on the servants gossiping about their masters.

CHAPELLE NOTRE-DAME-DE-BONSECOURS

This tiny ancient building is a monument to Marguerite Bourgeoys, a deeply pious woman dedicated to bringing Christian civilisation to New France. She founded a religious order, set up schools for both settlers and Indians, and built this church.

Church Marguerite Bourgeoys (► 12) picked the site for the chapel in 1657, just outside Ville-Marie's stockade, and persuaded Montreal's founder, Paul de Chomedey, Sieur de Maisonneuve, to help with the project. Legend has it that he helped cut the timber. The original building was destroyed by fire, and the present stone edifice dates from 1771. A 1998 renovation revealed some beautiful old 18th-century murals that had been covered up with more recent pictures.

Sailors The chapel has always had a special place in the hearts of mariners. Situated on the waterfront, it was built to house a statue of Notre-Dame-de-Bonsecours (Our Lady of Good Hope), credited with the rescue of those in peril at sea. A larger-than-life statue of the Virgin graces the steeple of the present building, facing the river with arms outstretched in welcome. Mariners who survived the perils of ocean crossings in the 18th and 19th centuries often came to the church to thank the Virgin for her help and to leave votive lamps in the shape of small model ships as tokens of appreciation. Many of them still hang from the ceiling and the chapel is usually referred to simply as the Église des Matelots, or the Sailors' Church. Visitors can climb the steeple to the 'aerial', a tiny chapel where mariners came to pray for safe passage. There is a museum, also renovated in 1998, where you can learn more about the life of Marguerite Bourgeoys.

HIGHLIGHTS

- Gold Madonna
- Murals
- Votive boats
- Mosaic inlays
- Madonna de Bonsecours
- 'Aerial'
- Views

INFORMATION

- ✚ G6
- ✉ 400 rue St-Paul Est
- ☎ 845 9991
- 🕐 May–Oct: Tue–Sun 9–4:30. Nov–Apr: Tue–Sun 10–3
- Ⓠ Champ-de-Mars
- 🚌 38
- ♿ Poor: four steps to church; no access to tower or museum
- 🎫 Church free. Museum inexpensive
- ↔ Château Ramezay (► 41), Lieu historique national Sir-G-E Cartier (► 42), Marché Bonsecours (► 44)
- ❓ Small gift shop

MARCHÉ BONSECOURS

HIGHLIGHTS

- Silver dome
- Portico
- Windows
- Columns
- Façade
- Grey-stone cladding

INFORMATION

- ✚ G6
- ✉ 350 rue Saint-Paul Est at rue Bonsecours
- ☎ 872 7730
- 🕐 Sat–Wed 10–6; Thu, Fri 10–9. Exhibition halls 10–6
- 🚇 Champ-de-Mars
- 🚌 38
- ♿ Excellent
- 🎟 Free
- ↔ Château Ramezay (➤ 41), Lieu historique national Sir-G-E Cartier (➤ 42), Chapelle Notre-Dame-de-Bonsecours (➤ 43), Vieux-Port de Montréal (➤ 45)

The silvery dome on top of the Marché Bonsecours has been a landmark on the Montréal waterfront for well over a century. It serves as a reminder of the city's importance as a busy port during the 19th century.

History The site of the Marché Bonsecours was an important one in 18th-century New France. Colonial authorities had an administrative centre here and the Marché Neuf, built to replace Montréal's first market in Place Royale, was nearby. The present building was never meant to serve as a market. The British erected it between 1845 and 1850 to fill cultural and political needs; the city councillors met downstairs and singers and musicians entertained the elite in the concert hall upstairs. It was only in 1878, when the mayor and councillors moved to their new home on rue Notre-Dame, that it became a market and remained one until the early 1960s. After a 1963 redevelopment scheme, the building served again as municipal offices until May 1996, when it reopened as a market.

Building The present grey-stone building is one of the most graceful in the city. Its long neoclassical façade, punctuated by rows of white-painted sash windows, stretches for two city blocks. The main portico, supported by six cast-iron Doric columns moulded in England, fronts on cobble-stoned rue Saint-Paul in the heart of the old city. The building is once again open to the public. Local artists and artisans display their wares in shops and stalls on the lower level and the upper floor is used for exhibits on Montréal's marine history and for concerts and banquets. The back door of the Marché opens on the Vieux-Port (➤ 45). In summer there is an outdoor café at street level.

A landmark on the Montréal waterfront

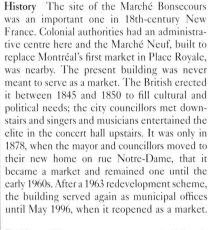

VIEUX-PORT DE MONTRÉAL

Imagination and federal money have transformed Montréal's old port from a tangle of rusting rail lines and crumbling warehouses into one of the city's most popular parks, with cycle trails, lawns, cafés and a new state-of-the-art science centre.

Seaways   Although Montréal is nearly 1,600 km from the sea, its position at the confluence of the Ottawa and St Lawrence Rivers made it an important trading port – a gateway to both the Great Lakes cities of Canada and the US and the fur-and-mineral-rich territory of the northwest. The old harbour bustled until the 1970s, when huge container ships rendered it obsolete. Shipping operations moved downriver and the port sank into decay.

Instant hit   Vieux-Port was popular from the day it opened as a park in 1992. In winter, the February Fête des Neiges attracts thousands of revellers, and the huge skating rink is always in use. In summer, the watefront promenade is alive with skateboarders, people out for a stroll, cyclists and street performers. You can hire bikes, roller blades and pedal-operated paddle boats. Private operators offer harbour cruises and jet-boat rides on the Lachine Rapids. A ferry takes foot passengers to the park on Île-Sainte-Hélène (➤ 46). The King Edward Pier is the home of iSci, Montréal's innovative science centre. It combines education (interactive science displays, exhibits on technology and two IMAX theatres), food (bistros and a family restaurant) and shopping (gift shop and outdoor market). At the eastern end of the port, visitors with good hearts can climb the 192 steps to the top of the Clock Tower – erected in memory of merchant mariners killed during World War I – for a fantastic view of the waterfront.

HIGHLIGHTS

- iSci
- Cinéma IMAX
- Jet boating
- La Tour de l'Horloge
- Harbour cruises
- People-watching

INFORMATION

- ✚ G7
- ✉ Access across old rail tracks at points along rue de la Commune
- ☎ 496 PORT or 873 2015
- 🕐 Varies with attraction
- 🍴 Place Jacques-Cartier, Maison des Éclusiers and Pointe-à-Callière
- Ⓜ Champ-des-Mars, Place-d'Armes, Square-Victoria
- 🚌 38, 55, 61, 129
- 🚻 Good
- 💷 Free access to site
- ↔ Basilique Notre-Dame (➤ 38), Centre d'histoire de Montréal (➤ 39), Pointe-à-Callière (➤ 40)
- ℹ Pavilion Jacques-Cartier, Quai Jacques-Cartier

23

ÎLE SAINTE-HÉLÈNE

HIGHLIGHTS

- Parkland
- Views
- La Ronde
- Old Fort
- Fireworks Competition
  (➤ 22)

Rustic calm meets urban energy on this beautiful island in the middle of the St Lawrence. Its quiet meadows and woodlands echo to the rattle of musket fire, the screams of roller-coaster riders and the amplified music of open-air concerts.

Top: at the David M
Stewart Museum
Above: Habitat 67

INFORMATION

- H7–J4
- Île Sainte-Hélène
- Information 872 4537
- La Biosphère (➤ 47), David M Stewart Museum (➤ 51), Île Notre-Dame (➤ 48), La Ronde (➤ 58)
- Île Ste-Hélène
- 167 Les Îles (summer only)
- Summer ferry from Quai Jacques-Cartier (Vieux-Port) ☎ 281 8000
- Variable depending on sight
- Variable depending on sight
- Vieux-Port de Montréal (➤ 45), La Biosphère (➤ 47)

Island Two things transformed Île Sainte-Hélène from an isolated offshore green space into a vibrant city park – the building of the Jacques Cartier Bridge in 1930 between the island and the city, and Expo '67, which opened the island to the world. To prepare for it, the city dumped tons of rubble from Métro excavations into the river to create space for pavilions, more than doubling the island's size.

Attractions One of the fair's flagship buildings – the geodesic dome that was the American pavilion – now encloses the Biosphère (➤ 47), an environmental interpretation centre. Other Expo leftovers include La Ronde, the amusement park, now bigger and better than in 1967, and containing one of the world's biggest roller-coasters, an amphitheatre used for open-air concerts and Alexander Calder's huge metal sculpture, *Man*; a man-made lake is the setting for a summer-long fireworks competition. On the Cité du Havre peninsula opposite the island is Moshe Safdie's block modular housing known as Habitat '67. One of the island's best attractions pre-dates the fair by more than 100 years. The Old Fort was built by the British after the War of 1812 with the Americans. Its barracks house the historical exhibits of the David M Stewart Museum and its parade square rattles to the musket drills of the Fraser Highlanders and the Compagnie Franche de la Marine – two 18th-century rivals now sharing one fort.

LA BIOSPHÈRE

There are two very good reasons for a visit to the Biosphère: to marvel at the shimmering geometric dome designed by Buckminster Fuller as the American Pavilion at Expo '67, and to see the centre's fascinating interactive displays about the environment.

Masterpiece   The Biosphère is relatively new – it opened only in 1995 – but it is framed by what is left of one of Expo '67's most enduring architectural landmarks. When Expo opened, the glittering sphere that housed the US pavilion was the world's biggest geodesic dome and one of the fair's most popular attractions. Afterwards, it housed an aviary and was known as the world's largest bird cage. But in 1976 fire destroyed the dome's acrylic skin, reducing the proud structure to a corroding metal skeleton.

New role   Today, displays inside highlight the ecosystems of the Great Lakes and St Lawrence River, a network of waterways that not only provides a vital lifeline for trade, but whose shores are also home to nearly half of Canada's population. Tours open in the Discovery Hall, where an eye-catching 5m globe helps explain the importance of water in our daily lives. In the Visions Hall, you enjoy views of the river and the city, while in the Connections Hall models, computers and diagrams demonstrate dramatically how we all share the same water as it falls as rain, runs through streams, is piped in and out of homes, and flows into the sea; you can also see the effect of pollution along the way. Take advantage of the soothing properties of water by bathing your feet (towels are provided).

HIGHLIGHTS

- Dome
- River views
- Globe
- Water theatre
- Satellite-fed data
- Interactive displays

INFORMATION

- 🔢 J6
- ✉ 160, chemin du Tour-de-Île, Île Sainte-Hélène
- ☎ 283 5000
- 🕐 Late Jun–early Sep: daily 10–6. Early Sep–late Jun: Tue–Sun 10–5
- 🚇 Île Ste-Hélène
- 🚌 167 Les Îles (summer only)
- ♿ Very good
- 💲 Moderate
- ↔ Île Sainte-Hélène (➤ 46), Île Notre-Dame (➤ 48)
- ❓ Guided tours, credit card bookings by phone

Discovery Hall's globe

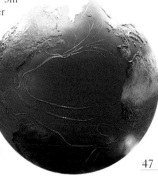

25

ÎLE NOTRE-DAME

HIGHLIGHTS

- Beach
- Views
- Floral Park
- Casino

INFORMATION

- K7–J5
- Île Notre-Dame Casino: 1 avenue du Casino
- Casino 392 2746 (or toll-free 1 800/665 2274 in Canada and the US). Beach 872 6211
- Casino daily 24 hours. Beach 23 Jun–27 Aug: daily 10–7 (if fine)
- Île Ste-Hélène
- 167 Les Îles (summer only)
- Summer ferry from Bassin Jacques-Cartier
- Variable
- Casino free. Beach moderate
- Île Sainte-Hélène (► 46), La Biosphère (► 47)
- Casino: visitors must be over 18; the wearing of shorts, leggings, t-shirts, track suit bottoms, beach-wear, running shoes and denim of any kind is not allowed

Before Expo '67, this long thin island hugging the south shore of the St Lawrence River didn't exist. Now it offers a huge variety of activities – car-racing, swimming, and gambling – as well as some magnificent views of the Montréal skyline.

Engineering If you bore a subway system through solid granite, you have to find somewhere to put all the rock you excavate. In the giddy days of the early 1960s, Montréal's visionary mayor Jean Drapeau decided to drop it in the middle of the St Lawrence River to create the venue for a world fair. He doubled the size of Île Sainte-Hélène (► 46) and created a brand-new island right next to it. Today the two islands form one park and when Drapeau died in 1999, the city named it Parc Jean-Drapeau.

Attractions The most popular attraction on the island, and one of the most popular in the city, is the Casino de Montréal. Its owner, the Québec provincial government, has tried to re-create the glamour of a European gambling palace in two spectacular buildings – the former French and Québec Expo '67 pavilions. Apart from its 3,000 slot machines and 118 tables, the casino also houses five restaurants and a cabaret-supper club. The island's second most popular attraction is the beach on the man-made lake. The only one within the city limits, it is kept clean by a unique filtration system that uses aquatic plants. The island is also home to the Circuit Gilles-Villeneuve, the only Formula 1 racing track in North America and home of the Air Canada Grand Prix. A vast floral park, built for the Floralies Internationales festival in 1980, is laced with canals and waterways, and filled with flowers, rose bushes and trees.

The popular Casino de Montréal

MONTRÉAL's *best*

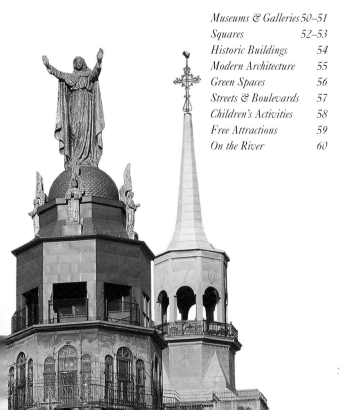

MUSEUMS & GALLERIES

Exhibits in the Musée des arts décoratifs

Museum pass

'La Carte-Musées Montréal' ☎ 845 6873 offers free admission to 19 of the city's leading museums including all those on these pages as well as all the sights and museums in the Top 25 Sights (except for those on pages 24–6).

CHÂTEAU DUFRESNE

The sumptuous interiors of these magnificent *beaux arts* homes, built in 1918 by Mario and Oscar Dufresne, offer a glimpse into the life of Montréal's French-speaking haute-bourgeoisie.
➕ G12 ✉ 2929 avenue Jeanne-d'Arc ☎ 872 2200 🕐 Thu–Sun 10–5 🚇 Pie-IX ♿ Good 💷 Moderate

DAVID M STEWART MUSEUM

Home to collections of firearms, maps, scientific instruments and domestic artefacts. Look in particular for the 18th-century kitchen.
➕ H5 ✉ Le Fort, Île Sainte-Hélène ☎ 861 6701 🕐 Mid-May–early Sep: daily 10–6. Early Sep–mid-May: Wed–Mon 10–5 🚇 Île Sainte-Hélène 🚌 167 ♿ Very poor 💷 Moderate

MUSÉE DES ARTS DÉCORATIFS

Ceramics, textiles, graphic arts and furniture from 1935 to the present make up this prestigious collection. The museum is linked to the Musée des beaux-arts (▶ 31).

🟥 E8 ✉ 2200 rue Crescent ☎ 284 1252 🕐 Tue, Thu–Sun 11–6; Wed 11–9 🚇 Guy-Concordia 🚌 24 ♿ Good 🎟 Free

MUSÉE JUSTE POUR RIRE

Film clips, stage sets, cartoons and costumes are used to trace the history of comedy. The museum also has a video café and performance space.

🟥 F6 ✉ 2111 boulevard Saint-Laurent ☎ 845 4000 🕐 Early Jun–early Sep: daily 11–8. Rest of the year: call for times 🍴 Café and gift shop 🚇 Saint-Laurent 🚌 24, 55

MUSÉE MARC-AURÈLE FORTIN

Self-taught Québec artist Marc-Aurèle Fortin (1888–1970) set out to create a whole new style of landscape painting, and was particularly fond of painting massive trees. Fortin also experimented with painting on grey or black backgrounds. This is the only museum dedicated to the work of one artist, though it sometimes shows work by other Québécois.

🟥 G7 ✉ 118 rue Saint-Pierre ☎ 845 6108 🕐 Tue–Sun 11–5 🚇 Square-Victoria (exit rue Saint-Jacques) 🚌 61 (57 peak hours) ♿ Poor: eight steps to main entrance 🎟 Moderate

MUSÉE DES HOSPITALIÈRES

This museum tells the story of Hôtel-Dieu, Montréal's first hospital, and the Hospitalières de Saint-Joseph, recruited in France in 1659 by Montréal's co-founder, Jeanne Mance, to run it, and captures something of the religious fervour of the age.

🟥 E6 ✉ 201 avenue des Pins ☎ 849 2919 🕐 Mid-Jun–mid-Oct: Tue–Fri 10–5; Sat, Sun 1–5. Mid-Oct–mid-Jun: Wed–Sun 1–5 🚇 Sherbrooke 🚌 144 ♿ Fair 🎟 Moderate

MAISON DE LA POSTE

The only philatelic centre in Canada devoted entirely to the sale of Canadian stamps.

🟥 F8 ✉ 1250 rue Université ☎ 846 5401 🕐 Mon–Fri 9–5:45 🚇 McGill 🚌 107 ♿ Good 🎟 Free

MAISON SAINT-GABRIEL

St Marguerite Bourgeoys ran a farm and school from this fine 17th-century farmhouse still standing among the tenements of Pointe-Saint-Charles. The house is full of tools, decorations, church vestments and furnishings from the period.

🟥 G10 ✉ 2146 Place Dublin ☎ 935 8136 🕐 Mid-Apr–mid-Dec: daily 9–5 🚇 Charlevoix 🚌 57 ♿ Fair 🎟 Moderate

Le Monde de Maurice Richard

No one played ice hockey more passionately than Maurice (Rocket) Richard who wore a Canadiens uniform from 1944 to 1960. He was the first player to score 50 goals in a season (which at that time was only 50 games long). This tiny museum pays him homage with pictures, jerseys, pucks and other artefacts.

🟥 G1 ✉ rue Pierre-de-Coubertin at Viau ☎ 251 9930 🕐 Tue–Sun 11–5 🚇 Viau ♿ Good 🎟 Free

Inspirational ice hockey player Maurice Richard

SQUARES

Nelson's Column

It seems odd that the statue of an English admiral should grace a square named for French explorer Jacques Cartier. Odder still that it should be French-speaking Sulpician priests who led the campaign to raise the monument to Horatio Nelson after his victory over a Franco-Spanish fleet in 1805 in the Napoleonic wars. The priests were anxious to show they were good subjects, and had little sympathy for the agnostic Corsican emperor.

Nelson's Column, overlooking Place Jacques-Cartier

PLACE D'ARMES

Place d'Armes was laid out at the end of the 17th century around the 'Gadoys' well, the main source of drinking water for Montréal's first French settlement. In the centre stands a statue (1895) of Paul de Chomedey Sieur de Maisonneuve, Montréal's founder, who is supposed to have killed an Iroquois chieftain on this spot in 1644. Around it lie the Basilique Notre-Dame (► 38), Séminaire Saint-Sulpice (► 54), the Banque de Montréal (► 54), the 1930 art deco Aldred Building, or Édifice Prevoyance (► 55) and the eight-storey Édifice New York Life (1888). To the south is the waterfront and Vieux-Port area (► 45).
✚ G7 🚇 Place d'Armes

SQUARE PHILLIPS

An immense, pigeon-spattered statue of King Edward VII, sculpted by Philippe Hébert in 1914, dominates this pleasant open space on rue Sainte-Catherine in the middle of the city centre. In summer, street vendors open stands at the king's feet, competing with the shops that surround the square. Across the street and slightly to the west is Christ Church Cathedral (► 33).
✚ F7 🚇 McGill

PLACE JACQUES-CARTIER

Right in the heart of Vieux-Montréal, this lovely cobbled square was created in 1804 as a municipal market; today its cafés, musicians, restaurants and quaint shops draw lively summer crowds. Nelson's Column (see panel) stands here and there are several fine 19th-century houses, including Maison del Vecchio, Maison Cartier and Maison Vandelac.
✚ G7 🚇 Champ-de-Mars

PLACE ROYALE

The city's oldest public square was once used as both a market and meeting-place between French settlers and native peoples. It was later the site of duels, whippings and public hangings.
✚ G7 🚇 Place-d'Armes

Elegant Victorian houses in square Saint-Louis

PLACE D'YOUVILLE

This Vieux-Port square, very pleasant when not full of cars, was landscaped over a dried-up creek bed during the 19th century, which is the reason for its strange shape. It housed a fish market at one stage, and was used by people meeting ships moored nearby.

✚ G7 🚇 Square-Victoria

SQUARE-DORCHESTER

This large green space in the city centre is lined with churches, historic buildings and office buildings. Just off rue Sainte-Catherine – the city's main shopping street – it is popular in summer with visitors and city workers alike. The main Infotouriste tourist office is here.

✚ F7–F8 🚇 Peel, Bonaventure

SQUARE SAINT-LOUIS

This leafy square was laid out in 1879, away from the centre and the Vieux-Port area, and is considered one of the city's finest. Its beautiful houses – formerly owned by Montréal's mercantile elite – are now home to poets, artists and writers attracted by the Bohemian atmosphere of the surrounding Saint-Denis district. At its southern end lies the pedestrian-only rue Prince-Arthur Est, full of street entertainers in summer.

✚ F6 🚇 Sherbrooke

The Faubourgs

Originally built almost entirely of wood, Montréal was constantly devastated by fires. In 1721 and 1727, two edicts made stone construction mandatory within the city walls. Those who could not afford stone began to build outside the city walls, thus creating Montréal's four 'faubourgs' (suburbs) – Saint-Laurent, Québec, Récollets and Saint-Louis. Here the houses had foundations and fireplaces of stone, but used timber for the walls and roofs.

53

HISTORIC BUILDINGS

*The ornate interior of the
Banque de Montréal*

BANQUE DE MONTRÉAL

The Bank of Montréal, Canada's oldest
financial institution, was founded in 1817.
Its headquarters moved 30 years later to
this neoclassical building inspired by
Rome's Pantheon. The bank has a small
museum displaying coins, mechanical
piggy banks and a cheque written on a
beaver pelt.

✚ G7 ✉ 119 rue Saint-Jacques ☎ 877 6892
🕐 Mon–Fri 10–4 🚇 Place-d'Armes 🚻 Good 💷 Free

MAISON PAPINEAU

This beautifully restored 18th-century
building was home to Louis-Joseph
Papineau (1786–1871), who played a
leading role in the French-Canadian
nationalist movement until the rebellion of
1837. Note the house's steeply banked roof,
designed to prevent the build-up of snow,
and the façade, much of which appears to
be rusticated (cut) stone but is actually
cleverly carved wood.

✚ G6 ✉ 440 rue Bonsecours ☎ None 🕐 Closed to the public
🚇 Champ-de-Mars 🚻 On a sloping and cobbled street

Oldest building

Montréal's oldest building is the
Séminaire St-Sulpice, closed to the
public but visible through the gate
to the west of the Basilique Notre-
Dame (➤ 36). It was built in
1685 for the Sulpicians, a Paris-
based order of priests, who were
proprietors of the entire island of
Montréal and who planned and
named many of the city's streets
and squares. The clock (1710)
over the main entrance is
reputedly North America's oldest
timepiece.

MAISON PIERRE-DU-CALVET

This fine 18th-century house was built in 1770
for Huguenot merchant Pierre du Calvet, who
was notorious for switching allegiance between
the French, British and Americans as each
controlled Montréal. Note the thick walls and
fireplaces, the windows with little squares of glass
imported from France, and the S-shaped brackets
on the façade, the only visible part of the bars
used to strengthen the internal wooden beams of
the building.

✚ G6 ✉ 401 rue Bonsecours ☎ 282 1725 🚇 Champ-de-Mars

VIEUX PALAIS DE JUSTICE

This impressive neoclassical courthouse, built in
1856, was used for almost a century to hear civil
cases. Most of it is now used for municipal offices,
but you can still admire the dome, exterior
columns and impressive portico.

✚ G7 ✉ 155 rue Notre-Dame Est 🚇 Champ-de-Mars

MODERN ARCHITECTURE

ÉDIFICE IBM-MARATHON

Designed in 1991 by New York's Kohn, Pederson, Fox, this 47-storey glass-and-granite tower is one of Montréal's most innovative.

➕ F8 ✉ 1250 boulevard René-Lévesque Ouest between rues Stanley and Drummond 🚇 Bonaventure

HABITAT '67

This angular 100-apartment complex was designed for Expo '67 by Moshe Safdie, one of the city's leading architects. The apartments are now some of the city's most sought-after.

➕ H7–H8 ✉ avenue Pierre-Dupuy, Cité du Havre 🚇 Place d'Armes ❓ Clearly visible from the Vieux-Port and Pointe-à-Callière

MAISON ALCAN

The Aluminum Company of Canada headquarters designed by Montréal architect Rag Affleck (1983) blends old and new and has a stunning atrium.

➕ E7 ✉ 1188 rue Sherbrooke Ouest ☎ 848 8000 ♿ Very good 🚇 Peel ❓ Guided tours, free lunch-time foyer concerts

PLACE VILLE-MARIE

This cruciform aluminium tower designed by I M Pei (completed in 1962) was Montréal's first modern skyscraper and is still one of the most distinctive buildings on the skyline. Its vast plaza is popular in summer and its street-level mall was the first element of the Underground City (► 34).

➕ F7 ✉ boulevard René-Lévesque between rues Mansfield and University 🚇 Bonaventure/McGill

TOUR BNP-BANQUE LAURENTIENNE

These twin blue-glass towers are eye-catching on the city centre skyline, dominating a particularly pleasant stretch of avenue McGill.

➕ E7 ✉ 1981 avenue McGill College 🚇 McGill

WESTMOUNT SQUARE

This black-metal and tinted-glass masterpiece by the eminent modernist architect Ludwig Mies van der Rohe dates from 1964.

➕ D9 ✉ rue Sainte-Catherine Ouest at avenue Greene 🚇 Atwater

Middle-aged

Fine Montréal buildings that are considered neither old nor new include the monolithic Édifice Sun Life (1914), reputed for many years to be the British Empire's largest building (✉ 1155 rue Metcalfe) and the Romanesque Windsor Station (1889), the former headquarters of the Canadian Pacific Railway (✉ Corner of rues Peel and de la Gauchetière).

The innovative Édifice IBM-Marathon (right)

Art deco

The Aldred Building, or Édifice Prevoyance (1928), is celebrated for its art-deco features (✉ 501–7 Place d'Armes). Édifice Ernest Cormier (1925), a grand neoclassical former courthouse, is now a centre for the performing arts (✉ 100 rue Notre-Dame Est).

GREEN SPACES

Viewpoints

For the best views, go to the Chalet terrace or the East Side Lookout off the Voie Camillien-Houde, both in the Parc du Mont-Royal (▶ 27); try L'Oratoire Saint-Joseph, at the city's highest point (▶ 28); climb up the little observatory in the Chapelle Notre-Dame-de-Bonsecours (▶ 43); or ride on the exciting tramway up the Olympic Stadium's famous tower (▶ 25).

PARC ANGRIGNON

This park has a small working farm, La Petite Ferme Angrignon, with guided tours and educational activities.

➕ Off map at A13 ✉ 3400 boulevard des Trinitaires ☎ 872 3816; La Petite Ferme Angrignon 872 1400 🕐 Park daily dawn to dusk. La Petite Ferme Angrignon early Jun–early Sep: daily 9–5 🚇 Angrignon ♿ Good 🎫 Free

PARC LAFONTAINE

Lafontaine divides into an English-style landscape in the west and a French-style garden in the east, with tennis courts, outdoor swimming pools and summer concerts.

➕ F4–F5 ✉ rue Sherbrooke Est between Saint-Hubert and Papineau 🕐 Daily 9AM–10PM 🍴 Snack bar 🚇 Sherbrooke (eight-block walk) ♿ Good 🎫 Free

PARC MAISONNEUVE

Parc Maisonneuve's slopes and frozen lakes are ideal for tobogganing, cross-country skiing and skating. You can picnic, walk, cycle and play golf in summer.

➕ F1–G1 ✉ 4601 rue Sherbrooke Est and boulevard Pie-XI ☎ 872 6555 🕐 Daily 9AM–10PM 🚇 Viau, Pie-IX ♿ Good 🎫 Park free. Golf course moderate

PARC WESTMOUNT

Said to be the loveliest city park, Westmount contains playing fields, a conservatory and an outstanding children's playground.

➕ D9–D10 ✉ rue Sherbrooke Ouest between Landsdowne and Melville ☎ None 🕐 Park daily 9AM–dusk. Conservatory usually daily 9–3 🍴 Cafés nearby 🚇 Place Saint-Henri, Vendôme ♿ Good

Parc Lafontaine

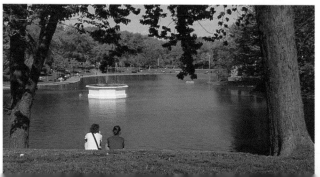

STREETS & BOULEVARDS

RUE BONSECOURS
A good example of the classical ideals of
Montréal's early French planners, with its fine
homes, notably No. 401 Maison Pierre-du-Calvet
and No. 440 Maison Papineau (both ➤ 54).
🞧 G6 🚇 Champ-de-Mars

AVENUE MCGILL COLLEGE
This short wide boulevard runs from Cathcart
near Place Ville-Marie up to McGill University's
Roddick Gates. If you stand on the Place Ville-
Marie plaza, you get a beautiful sweeping view of
the mountains and the campus framed by glass
office towers.
🞧 E7–F7 🚇 McGill

RUE SAINT-AMABLE
A narrow and lively
cobbled alley off Place
Jacques-Cartier, it is
notorious for the
many portrait artists vying for
business amid the
summer throng.
🞧 G7 🚇 Place-d'Armes

*The bright lights of rue
Sainte-Catherine*

RUE SAINTE-CATHERINE
Montréal's premier
shopping street, spoiled
in places by fast-food
outlets, is at its best between rues University and
Peel, and between rues de la Montagne, Crescent
and Bishop.
🞧 E8–F7 🚇 Guy-Concordia

RUE SAINT-DENIS
Rue Saint-Denis bisects Montréal's Quartier
Latin, a slightly seedy area that is now being
filled with interesting cafés, bistros and shops.
🞧 F6–G6 🚇 Berri-UQAM, Sherbrooke

RUE SAINT-PAUL
A block back from the waterfront, this is one of
the city's oldest and most fashionable streets,
with rather expensive cafés, restaurants and
fascinating speciality shops.
🞧 G6–G8 🚇 Place-d'Armes, Champ-de-Mars

RUE SHERBROOKE
The most interesting section of this major street
flanks an area whose residents were once
estimated to own 70 per cent of Canada's wealth.
You'll still find luxury shops, hotels and galleries.
🞧 E7–E8 🚇 Peel, McGill

The Main

Boulevard Saint-Laurent, or The
Main, still officially marks the
division between west and east in
the city. It housed Montréal's
earliest immigrants and today is
an incredibly varied ethnic and
cultural mix. Its surrounding
streets are full of bookshops, bric-
à-brac stores, second-hand clothes
shops and interesting bars, bistros
and restaurants.

57

CHILDREN'S ACTIVITIES

The Planétarium de Montréal is popular for its shows on the solar system

Kids' programmes

Most of the city's major museums have special programmes for children. The Musée des beaux-arts (➤ 31) offers hands-on creative programmes on Sunday mornings; the Canadian Centre for Architecture (➤ 32) has weekend toy-making workshops. The Redpath Museum at McGill University (➤ 29) has Sunday workshops to introduce children to science.

See Top 25 Sights for
LE BIODÔME (➤ 24)
PARC OLYMPIQUE (➤ 25)
ÎLE SAINTE-HÉLÈNE (➤ 46)
LE BIOSPHÈRE (➤ 47)
ÎLE NOTRE-DAME (➤ 48)

AQUADOME
This huge indoor fitness centre features three pools, one of them with water slides and sprinklers and full of different kinds of floats. There are plenty of places for parents to relax.
➕ Off map at A13 ✉ 1411 rue Lapierre (corner of boulevard de la Vérendrye), La Salle ☎ 367 5460 🕐 Daily 🚇 Agrignon, then bus No. 113 💵 Moderate

CIRQUE DU SOLEIL (➤ 80)

COSMODOME
The adventure of space exploration is the focus of this centre in surburban Laval, a 30-minute drive from the city centre. It's affiliated with the US Space Camp Foundation and is loaded with such kid-pleasing exhibits as replicas of rockets and space ships and a full-size mock-up of the space shuttle Endeavor. There are films – some of them shown on a 360-degree screen – as well as games and demonstrations.
➕ Off map at A3 ✉ 2150 Autoroute de Laurentides, Laval ☎ 978 3615 or 800/565 CAMP 🕐 24 Jun–1 Sep: daily 10–6. 2 Sep–23 Jun: Tue–Sun 10–6 💵 Expensive

PLANÉTARIUM DE MONTRÉAL
Regular shows in the big domed theatre offer guided tours to our solar system and more distant galaxies. Themed programmes that alter every few months explore space collisions, black holes, sun spots, eclipses and the star that guided the Magi to Bethlehem.
➕ F8 ✉ 1000 rue Saint-Jacques Ouest ☎ 872 4530 🕐 24 Jun–Labour Day: daily. Labour Day–23 Jun: Tue–Sun 💵 Moderate

FREE ATTRACTIONS

Free and almost free

Watch the world go by in a pavement café, amble around the Vieux-Port, linger with the night-time crowds on rue Sainte-Catherine Ouest and Saint-Denis or try the multi-ethnic shops and markets of The Main on a Saturday morning. To enjoy street performers, head for the Vieux-Port or the pedestrian-only rue Prince-Arthur Est.

PARKS

Look for free concerts in summer in Montréal's parks (► 56). In the Parc du Mont-Royal, you can enjoy great views of the city centre and listen to the Montréal Symphony Orchestra's summer performances alongside Lac-aux-Castors (Beaver Lake). The Îles Sainte-Hélène and Notre-Dame (► 46, 48) are also lively in summer.

MUSEUMS

Several of the city's larger museums have one free late-evening admittance each week. At present there is no admittance charge for the McCord Museum from 6 to 9 on Thursdays (► 30) or for the permanent collection at the Musée des beaux-arts (► 31), while the main collection of the Musée d'art contemporain is free on Wednesdays between 6 and 9 and for some weekend programmes (► 36). There is no charge for The Banque du Montréal (► 54), the Maison de la Poste (► 50) and the Redpath Museum (► 29).

CONCERTS AND FESTIVALS

Oratoire Saint-Joseph (► 28) has free organ recitals on Wednesday evenings in summer and carillon concerts from Wednesday to Saturday all year round. The atrium of the Maison Alcan (► 55) regularly hosts free lunch-time concerts. Admission to noon and evening organ and choral concerts in Christ Church Cathedral (► 33) is by donation. The famous Jazz and Juste Pour Rire festivals (► 22) have many outdoor shows open to all. Free concerts take place at the Vieux-Port in summer and there is an open-air theatre in Parc Lafontaine (► 56).

People-watching is one of Montréal's favourite free entertainments

ON THE RIVER

Cruise for less

In summer, the ferry trip from the Vieux-Port to Longueuil across the St Lawrence makes a great quick getaway on the water – and the price is right. The boat stops at La Ronde on the Île Sainte-Hélène. Frequencies vary, but it runs hourly between 10AM and 1AM in each direction in July and August.

➕ G7 ✉ Departs Quai Jacques-Cartier ☎ 281 8000 🕐 Mid-May–mid-Oct

Croisières Nouvelle-Orléans paddle steamer

BATEAU-MOUCHE

Take a trip on this glass-topped boat that explores the St Lawrence and its islands. They also operate dinner cruises. Le Canard Malard, a large inflatable operated by the same company, offers ecological and historical trips.

➕ G7 ✉ Quai Jacques-Cartier ☎ Bateau Mouche 849 9952 or toll-free 1 800/361 9952 in Canada and the US. Le Canard Malard 285 8848 or 565 5815 🕐 Early May–early Oct: daily at 10, noon, 2, 4; dinner cruise at 7PM. Le Canard Malard: Île Grosbois daily at 10, 1, 4; sunset cruise at 7PM 🚇 Champ-de-Mars ♿ Good 💲 Expensive

CROISIÈRES NOUVELLE-ORLÉANS

Cruise the St Lawrence and islands aboard a Mississippi-style paddle steamer.

➕ G7 ✉ Quai Jacques-Cartier ☎ 842 7655 or toll-free 1 800/ 667 3131 in Canada and the US 🕐 Cruises mid-May–mid-Oct: daily at noon, 2, 4; dinner-dance cruise 7PM 🚇 Champ-de-Mars ♿ Good 💲 Expensive

CROISIÈRES DÉCOUVERTES DU PORT

Take a two-hour cruise, a dinner-dance cruise around Montréal or a day trip to the Îles de Sorel, 48km down river.

➕ H6 ✉ Quai de l'Horloge at rue Bonsecours ☎ 842 3871 or toll-free 1 800/667 3131 in Canada and the US 🕐 Island Discovery mid-May–mid-Oct: daily at noon, 2:30. Îles de Sorel mid-Jun–early Sep: daily at 8AM 🚇 Champ-de-Mars ♿ Good 💲 Expensive

SAUTE-MOUTONS

Shoot the Lachine Rapids aboard open hydrofoil-type boats or by speed-boat.

➕ G7 ✉ Office: 105 rue de la Commune. Departures: Saute-Moutons at Quai de L'Horloge; Jet Saint-Laurent at Quai Jacques-Cartier ☎ 284 9607 🕐 Saute-Moutons May–Sep: daily every 2 hours 10–6. Jet Saint-Laurent May–Sep: daily every 30 minutes 10–7 🚇 Champ-de-Mars ♿ Very good 💲 Very expensive. Booking required; no children allowed under 6

MONTRÉAL
where to...

FRENCH

Prices

Expect to pay for a meal per person, excluding drinks, service charge and federal and provincial taxes (which amount to just over 15 per cent):

£	up to $18
££	up to $35
£££	more than $35

If you are watching your budget, consider dining at a restaurant that allows you to bring your own wine. Entries are designated as 'BYOB', bring your own bottle (► 63).

À LA DÉCOUVERTE (££)

Classic French cuisine on a quiet residential street in the Plateau Mont-Royal. Reserve two weeks in advance for weekends. BYOB.

🚼 E4 ✉ 4354 avenue Christophe-Colombe ☎ 529 8377 🕓 Tue–Sun dinner 🚇 Mont-Royal 🅿 Booking essential

AU BISTRO GOURMET (££)

Classic bistro food: mussels in pullet sauce, kidney in dijonaise sauce, pear trottoir.

🚼 E8 ✉ rue Saint-Mathieu ☎ 846 1553 🕓 Mon–Fri lunch, dinner; Sat, Sun dinner

AU PETIT RESTO (££)

A relaxed BYOB, with good value French food. Tables are more spacious in the front, more intimate in the back. Dressier at weekends.

🚼 E4 ✉ 4650 rue Mentana ☎ 589 7963 🕓 Tue–Sun dinner 🚇 Laurier/Mont-Royal 🅿 Booking required

BEAVER CLUB (£££)

An elegant French restaurant that started in the 19th century as a private club for fur merchants.

🚼 F7 ✉ Hôtel La Reine Élizabeth, 900 boulevard René-Lévesque Ouest at rue Mansfield ☎ 861 3511 🕓 Mon–Fri lunch, dinner; Sat, Sun dinner 🚇 Bonaventure 🅿 Book; jacket and tie required

BISTRO L'ENTREPONT (££)

Widely considered the best BYOB, perfect for a romantic French dinner. Dress up.

🚼 D5 ✉ 4622 avenue de l'Hotel-de-Ville ☎ 845 1369 🕓 Daily dinner (two sittings at 6 and 9) 🚇 Mont-Royal 🅿 Booking essential

BONAPARTE (£££)

Sit in the fireplace room overlooking rue Saint-Sacrement and you'll swear you're in Paris.

🚼 G7 ✉ 443 rue Saint-François-Xavier ☎ 844 4368 🕓 Mon–Fri lunch, dinner; Sat, Sun dinner 🚇 Place d'Armes 🅿 Book in summer

LE CAFÉ DE PARIS (£££)

Classic French food, rarefied ambience and affluent clientele. Delightful courtyard garden in summer.

🚼 E7 ✉ Hôtel Ritz-Carlton, 1228 rue Sherbrooke Ouest ☎ 842 4212 🕓 Mon–Sat breakfast, lunch, tea and dinner; Sun tea and dinner 🚇 Peel 🅿 Book; jacket required for lunch and dinner

LE CAVEAU (££)

Unadorned French cooking in a three-storey town house; upper levels are more airy.

🚼 E7 ✉ 2063 rue Victoria between rue Sherbooke Ouest and avenue du Présidente-Kennedy ☎ 844 1624 🕓 Daily lunch, dinner 🚇 McGill 🅿 Book

LES CAPRICES DE NICHOLAS (£££)

The atrium garden of this prettily decorated, three-room restaurant is the perfect place for truffle-scented warm quail and spinach salad.

🚼 E8 ✉ 2072 rue Drummond ☎ 282 9790 🕓 Tue–Fri lunch, dinner; Sat, Mon dinner 🚇 Peel 🅿 Booking required

CHEZ LA MÈRE MICHEL (£££)

Conservative but perfect dishes – lobster soufflé Mantua and bison and caribou in season – at this established city centre restaurant.
✚ E8 ✉ 1209 rue Guy ☎ 934 0473 🕐 Daily lunch, dinner 🚇 Guy/Concordia
❓ Booking recommended

CLAUDE POSTEL (£££)

Superb French provincial cooking and sensational desserts.
✚ G7 ✉ 443 rue Saint-Vincent ☎ 875 5067
🕐 Mon–Fri lunch, dinner; Sat, Sun dinner 🚇 Champs-de-Mars
❓ Booking recommended

LA LOUX (££)

Classic French food with a modern edge in a discreet, elegant setting.
✚ E6 ✉ 250 avenue des Pins Est ☎ 287 9127 🕐 Mon–Fri lunch, dinner; Sat, Sun dinner
🚇 Sherbrooke ❓ Booking recommended

LE PASSE PARTOUT (£££)

New York-born chef James MacGuire makes the trek out to this West End restaurant well worth it. He bakes the best bread in Montréal.
✚ B10 ✉ 3857 boulevard Décarie ☎ 487 7750 🕐 Thu, Fri lunch, dinner; Sat dinner; Tue, Wed lunch 🚇 Villa Maria
❓ Booking essential

LE PÉGASE (££)

Unpretentious neighbourhood place – try calf brains with spinach and almonds, caribou chop with sun-dried tomatoes. BYOB.
✚ G5 ✉ 1831 rue Gilford ☎ 522-0487 🕐 Tue–Sat dinner 🚇 Papineau 🚍 45
❓ Booking recommended

LES HALLES (£££)

Long wine list, classic French cuisine. Less formal bistros.
✚ E8 ✉ 1450 rue Crescent ☎ 844 2328 🕐 Tue–Fri lunch, dinner; Mon, Sat dinner 🚇 Peel ❓ Booking recommended

LES REMPARTS (£££)

Dimly lit and romantic cellar restaurant.
✚ G7 ✉ 97 rue de la Commune Est ☎ 392 1649
🕐 Tue–Sun lunch, dinner
🚇 Place d'Armes ❓ Booking recommended

L'EXPRESS (££)

Elbow-to-elbow tables, cheerfully frantic service, perfect food, interesting wines.
✚ E5 ✉ 3927 rue Saint-Denis at rue Duluth ☎ 845 5333
🕐 Mon–Sat lunch, dinner; Sun dinner 🚇 Sherbrooke
❓ Booking required

RESTAURANT JULIEN (££)

Fashionable city centre restaurant with a canopied terrace in summer.
✚ F7 ✉ 1191 rue Union ☎ 871 1581 🕐 Mon–Fri lunch, dinner; Sat dinner
❓ Booking recommended

TOQUÉ! (£££)

Chef Normand Laprise is a celebrity. His ingredients are Québécois, the discipline French, and the accent decidedly contemporary.
✚ F6 ✉ 3842 rue Saint-Denis ☎ 499 2084 🕐 Daily dinner
🚇 Sherbrooke ❓ Booking essential

Bring your own bottle

Restaurants where you 'Bring Your Own Bottle ' (*Apporter son vin*) are common in Montréal, thanks to a quirk in Québec's provincial liquor laws. The food quality in these places ranges from pedestrian to excellent, but they are usually inexpensive. The restaurants sell no alcohol themselves, but they will gladly open your wine or beer and provide glasses. BYOBs first sprang up on rue Prince-Arthur Est, and spread to the streets around rue Duluth. Better places, however, can be found around rue Mentana and around avenues Mont-Royal and Marie-Anne, and in the gay village (Le Village) around rues Amherst and Ontario. Inexpensive wine can be bought at local shops (*dépanneurs*). Better wine is available at outlets of the Société des Alcools du Québec.

ECLECTIC & CONTEMPORARY

Multi ethnic flavours

French cuisine in all its forms – provincial, bourgeois, classic and updated – dominates Montréal's dining scene, although contemporary 'fusion fare', which draws on many ethnic flavours, has not taken hold as it has in California and New York. More than 30 different ethnic groups are also represented in Montréal. The Greek and Italian immigrants who poured into the city in the latter half of the 20th century have established an enduring place in Montréalers' stomachs. Cantonese cooking has been a presence since Chinese railway workers established a foothold in the city in the late 1800s; refugees from Indochina, who began arriving in the city in the late 70s, opened Vietnamese restaurants and noodle shops. The current craze is for Thai food.

BAZOU (££)
The name means 'jalopy'; in keeping with the theme, the rabbit's creamy mushroom sauce is called Mustang sauce.
✚ F6 ✉ 1310 boulevard de Maisonneuve Est ☎ 526 4940 ⊕ Mon–Sat lunch, dinner ⍟ Beaudry

LA CHRONIQUE (£££)
No-one blends the flavours of Europe, America and Asia as seamlessly as Chef Marc de Cank in dishes such as bok choy sweetbreads and wild-mushroom salsa. Pecan pie with Jack Daniel's and passion fruit soufflé are worth saving room for.
✚ D5 ✉ 99 avenue Laurier Ouest ☎ 271 3095 ⊕ Tue–Fri lunch, dinner; Sat dinner ⍟ Laurier ▯ 51

GLOBE (£££)
Even the sleek, trendy decor is not as daring as the cooking – note the Québec foie gras pot-roasted with plum wine.
✚ F6 ✉ 3455 boulevard Saint-Laurent ☎ 284 3823 ⊕ Daily dinner ⍟ Saint-Laurent ▯ 55

GINGER (££)
Have a saki martini, then tuck into chicken ramen or tuna with vermicelli. Bruce Lee videos in the corner; young and hip.
✚ E6 ✉ 16 avenue des Pins Est ☎ 844 2121 ⊕ Daily dinner ⍟ Sherbrooke

MAÎKO SUSHI (££)
What happens when Japan meets Italy in North America? You get sushi pizza with a fried-rice crust and toppings of smoked salmon and shallots.
✚ C5 ✉ 387 rue Bernard Ouest ☎ 490 1225 ⊕ Mon–Fri lunch, dinner; Sat, Sun dinner ⍟ Rosemont (taxi recommended)

MEDITERRANEO (£££)
Sandstone floors and a huge window set off some of the trendiest food in the city.
✚ F6 ✉ 3500 boulevard Saint-Laurent ☎ 844 0027 ⊕ Daily dinner ⍟ Saint-Laurent

LE MONKLAND (££)
Serves such decidedly fashionable food as grilled-vegetable sand-wiches, spinach salad with goat's cheese and marinated lamb tartar.
✚ B10 ✉ 5555 avenue Monkland ☎ 486 5786 ⊕ Mon–Fri lunch, dinner; Sat, Sun dinner ⍟ Villa-Maria ▯ 103, 162

SOCIÉTÉ CAFÉ (£££)
The lobby restaurant in the fashionable Hôtel Vogue offers such eclectic specials as crab and avocado *tian* and braised pork with green and yellow tomato salsa.
✚ E8 ✉ 1415 rue de la Montagne ☎ 987 8168 ⊕ Daily breakfast, lunch, dinner ⍟ Peel

ZEN (££–£££)
Dishes blend Szechuan, Thai, Indonesian and Malaysian flavours. The fixed-price Zen Experience allows you to pick what you want from 40 offerings.
✚ E7 ✉ 1050 rue Sherbrooke Ouest ☎ 499 0801 ⊕ Daily lunch, dinner ⍟ Peel

ITALIAN & GREEK

BUONA NOTTE (££)

Modern and sophis-
ticated. Serves excellent
risotto and grilled fish.
➕ E6 ✉ 3518 boulevard
Saint-Laurent ☎ 848 0644
🕐 Mon–Sat lunch, dinner; Sun
dinner 🚇 Mont-Royal 🚌 9, 55

DA EMMA (££)

Charming old building
overlooking the Vieux-
Port. Try the fettucine
with porcini mushrooms
or roast baby pig.
Helpful service.
➕ G7 ✉ 777 rue de la
Commune Ouest ☎ 392 568
🕐 Mon–Fri lunch, dinner; Sat
dinner 🚇 Square Victoria
❓ Booking for dinner

EDUARDO (££)

Reliable and inexpen-
sive pastas plus meat and
seafood dishes. Cramped,
often busy; brisk and
efficient service.
➕ E5 ✉ 404 rue Duluth Est
☎ 843 3330 🕐 Mon–Fri
lunch, dinner; Sat, Sun dinner
🚇 Sherbrooke/Mont-Royal

LA FORNARINA (££)

A good inexpensive
family-run choice, in
Montréal's Little Italy.
Tasty, basic pastas,
seafood and meat
dishes, as well as thin
crust pizzas cooked in a
wood-fired brick oven.
➕ B4 ✉ 6825 boulevard
Saint-Laurent ☎ 271 141
🕐 Mon–Sat dinner; Sat,
Sun dinner 🚇 Castenau, Jean-
Talon ❓ Bookings needed
weekends

LE JARDIN
DE PANOS (££)

The best of the Greek
eateries in the rue
Duluth area, with good
versions of standard
dishes such as calamari
and moussaka.
➕ E5 ✉ 521 rue Duluth Est
☎ 521 4206 🕐 Daily lunch,
dinner 🚇 Sherbrooke, Mont-
Royal

LE LATINI (£££)

Lavish Italian restaurant
with a terrace for *alfresco*
summer dining.
➕ F7 ✉ 1130 rue Jeanne-
Mance ☎ 831 3166
🕐 Mon–Fri lunch; Sat dinner
🚇 Place-d'Armes, Place-des-Arts
❓ Booking required

MILOS (£££)

One of the most
beautiful and priciest
restaurants in the city.
Exquisite Greek seafood.
➕ D5 ✉ 5357 avenue du
Parc ☎ 272 3522 🕐 Mon–Fri
lunch, dinner; Sat, Sun dinner
❓ Booking required; taxi
advised

IL MULINO (££)

Small, always-booked
restaurant on the edge
of Little Italy. A family
affair with wonderful
antipasti – olive-rich
focaccia bread, grilled
hot peppers, stuffed
aubergine, grilled
portobello mushrooms
with cheese.
➕ C4 ✉ 236 rue Saint-
Zotique Est ☎ 273 5776
🕐 Tue–Sun lunch, dinner
🚇 Beaubien ❓ Booking
essential

PSAROTAVERNA DU
SYMPOSIUM (££)

Fish nets and lots of
blue and white paint,
plus grilled fresh fish,
shrimp and octopus.
➕ E5 ✉ 4293 rue Saint-Denis
☎ 842 0867 🕐 Mon–Fri
lunch, dinner; Sat, Sun dinner
🚇 Mont-Royal

The food of
pioneers

One of the hardest things to find
in Montréal is the hearty
Québécois food the French
pioneers developed to help them
survive harsh winters and hard-
working summers — thick pea
soup, spicy *tourtière* (a kind of
meat pie), pigs' feet, game pie,
meatball stew and heavy, syrup-
soaked desserts like sugar pie
and *pudding au chomeur*
(literally 'unemployed pudding').
Two unpretentious places that
offer these delicacies are the
Binerie Mont Royal (✉ 367
avenue Mont-Royal Est ☎ 285
9078) and Chez Clo (✉ 3199
rue Ontario Est ☎ 522 5348).

PAN-ASIAN

Popular mess

Québec's very own contribution to the fast-food culture is something called *poutine* (literally 'mess'). It consists of a big dish of French fries, covered liberally with cottage cheese and drowned in a gelatinous mass of thick, brown, beef gravy. Another fast-food favourite is barbecued chicken, a crispy-skinned, spit-roasted bird served with a spicy sauce. The man who dreamed up the concept and helped design the rotisserie is Swiss-born Marcel Mauron, who opened the Chalet Bar-B-Q in 1944. The Chalet's chicken is still the best (✚ C10 ✉ 5456 rue Sherbrooke Ouest ☎ 489 7235), but the ubiquitous Saint-Hubert chain (named for the street where it started) also offers a presentable version (✚ E5 ✉ 4462 rue Saint-Denis ✉ 844 9521).

BON BLÉ RIZ (££)
Lamb in a peppery anise-flavoured sauce and spicy shrimp are among the flamboyant dishes at this unpretentious restaurant.
✚ F6 ✉ 1437 boulevard Saint-Laurent ☎ 844 1447 🕐 Mon–Fri lunch, dinner; Sat, Sun dinner 🚇 Saint-Laurent

CHAO PHRAYA (£)
A Thai favourite, with over 100 dishes.
✚ D5 ✉ 50 boulevard Laurier Ouest at rue Saint-Urbain ☎ 272 5339 🕐 Sat–Wed dinner; Thu, Fri lunch, dinner 🚌 29

CHU CHAI (££)
This vegetarian paradise whips up fine renditions of Thai favourites with substituted soy or seitan for chicken and shrimp.
✚ D5 ✉ 4088 rue Saint-Denis ☎ 843 4194 🕐 Daily lunch, dinner 🚇 Sherbrooke, Mont-Royal

ESCALA A SÀIGON (££)
The French ruled Saigon for decades, and it shows in the Escale's anise-flavoured sliced eel and crêpes stuffed with steamed rice.
✚ D5 ✉ 107 avenue Laurier Ouest ☎ 272 3456 🕐 Daily lunch, dinner 🚇 Laurier

MIKADO (££)
The sushi's good and the excellent cooked food includes such delicacies as soft-shelled crabs in ginger and grilled eel.
✚ D5 ✉ 368 avenue Laurier Ouest ☎ 279 4809 🕐 Mon–Fri lunch, dinner; Sat, Sun dinner 🚇 Laurier 🚌 51

ORCHIDÉEDE CHINE (£££)
Best of the Tuxedo Chinese restaurants – flash-fried spinach and dumpling with peanut sauce served in an elegantly simple setting.
✚ E7 ✉ 2017 rue Peel ☎ 287 1878 🕐 Mon–Fri lunch, dinner; Sat dinner 🚇 Peel

PEMENT ROUGE (£££)
High ceilings and crystal chandeliers form an Edwardian backdrop for Szechuan dishes like shredded lamb in spiced sauce and steamed fish in ginger.
✚ F8 ✉ 1170 rue Peel ☎ 866 7816 🕐 Mon–Fri lunch, dinner; Sat, Sun dinner 🚇 Peel, Bonaventure

SOUVENIRS DE BANGKOK (££)
Friendly, family-owned restaurant. The seafood dishes are best – try sautéed squid with crunchy spinach and peanuts, or shrimp and cucumber chiffon with mint. Vegetarians can feast heartily on coconut-milk and vegetables with green curry. BYOB.
✚ E8 ✉ 1925 rue Sainte-Catherine Ouest ☎ 938 2235 🕐 Mon–Fri lunch, dinner; Sat, Sun dinner 🚇 Guy-Concordia

SOUVENIRS DE L'INDOCHINE (£)
Sesame seeds add crunch to beef cutlets and chilli peppers spice the chicken at this Vietnamese favourite.
✚ E5 ✉ 243 avenue Mont-Royal Ouest ☎ 848 0336 🕐 Mon–Fri lunch, dinner; Sat, Sun dinner 🚇 Mont-Royal 🚌 97

OTHER ETHNIC CUISINES

L'ACTUEL (££)
This noisy city centre café does Belgian specialities best, offering several variations on the theme of mussels and French fries.
⊞ F8 ✉ 1194 rue Peel ☎ 866 1537 🕐 Mon–Fri lunch, dinner; Sat dinner 🚇 Peel, Bonaventure

EL AMIGO (££)
Guitar-players wander from table to table on weekends and the menu draws from all over Central America.
⊞ B4 ✉ 51 rue Saint-Zotique Est ☎ 278 4579 🕐 Daily lunch, dinner 🚇 de Castelnau 🚌 55

BYBLOS (£)
Books and Scrabble games provide a backdrop for such Iranian dishes as spinach yoghurt and chicken koukou.
⊞ E4 ✉ 1499 avenue Laurier Est ☎ 523 9396 🕐 Tue–Sun lunch, dinner 🚇 Laurier 🚌 27

LA GAZELLE (££)
Chorba soup, royal couscous and desserts rich in dates and nuts mark this North African restaurant.
⊞ E5 ✉ rue Rachel Est ☎ 843 9598 🕐 Daily dinner 🚇 Mont-Royal

JANO (££)
This Portuguese grill produces delectable lamb chops, sardines, trout, and sausages dabbed with a little pepper oil.
⊞ F6 ✉ 3883 boulevard Saint-Laurent ☎ 849 0646 🕐 Daily dinner 🚇 Saint-Laurent 🚌 55

PUCAPUCA (£)
Rabbit with roasted peanuts and quail in mango sauce highlight owner Ciro Wong's Peruvian menu.
⊞ D5 ✉ 5400 boulevard Saint-Laurent ☎ 272 8029 🕐 Tue–Sat dinner 🚇 Laurier

SENZALA (££)
Orange walls and samba music provide the backdrop for such Brazilian specialities as squid in garlic and *mariscada* (fish, clams and pork in a white-wine sauce).
⊞ C5 ✉ 177 avenue Bernard Ouest ☎ 274 1464 🕐 Mon–Fri lunch, dinner; Sat, Sun brunch, dinner 🚌 55

SIRÈNE DE LA MER (££)
Pick your main dish from the fish market next door; eat it grilled with a selection of Lebanese salads.
⊞ A6 ✉ 114 Dresden ☎ 345 0345 🕐 Daily lunch, dinner 🚇 Acadie (cab recommended)

CAFÉ STASH (££)
Here you sit on old pews to consume Polish specialities – hot borscht, pierogi and several kinds of sausage.
⊞ G7 ✉ rue Saint-Paul Ouest ☎ 845 6611 🕐 Daily lunch, dinner 🚇 Place d'Armes

TROIKA (£££)
Plenty of caviar, smoked and marinated fish, blinis, black bread, and flavoured, frozen vodkas.
⊞ E7 ✉ 2171 rue Crescent ☎ 849 9333 🕐 Daily dinner; Wed–Fri lunch 🚇 Guy-Concordia

Cheap eats
Try the food courts in Central Station, Place Ville-Marie and Complex Desjardins for an inexpensive hot or cold lunch of anything from muffins and smoked meat sandwiches to burgers, lasagne and beef noodles. Little shops selling huge bowls of Vietnamese noodle soup have sprung up along the southern end of boulevard Saint-Laurent just north of rue Viger. They're good value, filling and tasty.

STEAKS & DELI FOOD

Smoked meat and bagels

Jewish refugees from Eastern Europe – primarily Romania – started arrivng in the city in great numbers in the early decades of the 20th century. Like all other immigrants, they brought their food. Two such delicacies that have become an integral part of Montréal diet are bagels (a very crusty version, baked in a wood-burning oven) and smoked meat, which is served thin-sliced and heaped in rye-bread sandwiches. The meat is beef brisket that has been dry-cured in spices for a few weeks and then smoked for several hours. Former Montréalers of all ethnic backgrounds usually stock up on both these foods during visits home. For smoked meat they usually go to Schwartz's (see main entry this page) and for bagels it's either Saint-Viateur Bagel Shop (✉ 263 rue Saint-Viateur ☎ 276 8044) or Fairmount Bagel Factory (✉ 74 rue Fairmount Ouest ☎ 272 0667).

BENS (£)
Opened in 1908 by Ben Kravitz, still run by his grandsons, and packed day and night with Montréalers. Try the Big Ben sandwich and the strawberry cheesecake. The 1930s setting is a real winner.
✚ E7 ✉ 990 boulevard de Maisonneuve Ouest at Metcalfe ☎ 844 1000 ⏰ Daily breakfast, lunch, dinner. Until 5AM 🚇 McGill

ENTRECÔTE SAINT-JEAN (£)
Bistro decor with a simple and inexpensive menu – walnut salad, sirloin, perfectly crunchy fries and chocolate profiteroles.
✚ F7 ✉ 2022 rue Peel ☎ 281 6492 ⏰ Daily dinner; Mon–Fri lunch 🚇 Peel

GIBBYS (£££)
This huge stone-walled dining room in Vieux-Montréal features steak and seafood.
✚ G7 ✉ 298 place d'Youville ☎ 282 1837 ⏰ Daily dinner from 4:30PM 🚇 Place Victoria ❓ Booking recommended

THE MAIN (£)
Good neighbourhood deli with excellent smoked meat.
✚ E5 ✉ 3864 boulevard Saint-Laurent ☎ 843 8126 ⏰ Daily breakfast, lunch, dinner 🚇 Mont-Royal

MR STEER (£)
An unpretentious steakhouse with leatherette booths that serves the juiciest and tastiest burgers in the city centre.
✚ E8 ✉ 1198 rue Saint-Catherine Ouest ☎ 866 3233 ⏰ Daily lunch, dinner 🚇 Peel

MAGNAN (££)
This working-class tavern serves roast beef, steaks and salmon pie to dockers, lorry drivers, lawyers and executives. On the Lachine Canal bicycle path.
✚ F9 ✉ 2602 rue Saint-Patrick ☎ 935 9647 ⏰ Daily lunch, dinner 🚇 Charlevoix

MOISHE'S (£££)
Marbled steaks aged the same way since 1938. Crowded and noisy.
✚ E6 ✉ 3961 boulevard Saint-Laurent at rue Duluth ☎ 845 3509 ⏰ Daily dinner 🚇 Mont-Royal

SCHWARTZ'S (£)
The three best things on the menu here are smoked meat, smoked meat and smoked meat – but the steaks are pretty good, too. Famous and packed – expect brusque service and queues.
✚ E5 ✉ 3895 boulevard Saint-Laurent at rue Napoléon ☎ 842 4813 ⏰ Daily lunch, dinner 🚇 Mont-Royal

WILENSKY'S LIGHT LUNCH (£)
Made famous by novelist Mordecai Richler and little-changed since 1932. Try the sandwich 'special' – salami and bologna on a roll with cheese.
✚ D5 ✉ 34 avenue Fairmount Ouest at rue Clark ☎ 271 0247 ⏰ Mon–Fri lunch and take-out 9–4 🚇 Laurier

CAFÉS & PÂTISSERIES

AMBIANCE (£)
This quirky, antique-stuffed place on Antique Row serves salads, sandwiches and imaginatively sauced pastas. Busy at lunch.
✚ F8 ✉ 1874 rue Notre-Dame Ouest ☎ 939 2609 🕐 Wed–Sat 11–5; Sun–Tue 11–4:40PM. Jan, Feb: closed Sat. Dinner by arrangement only 🚇 Lucien-l'Allier

L'ANECDOTE (£)
This neighbourhood spot, hung with film posters and old Coke ads, specialises in vegetarian sandwiches.
✚ E5 ✉ 801 rue Rachel Est, near rue Saint-Hubert ☎ 526 7967 🕐 Daily breakfast, lunch, dinner 🚇 Mont-Royal

CALORIES (£)
All kinds of flavoured cheesecakes and chocolate cakes. Excellent coffee.
✚ E10 ✉ rue Sainte-Catherine Ouest ☎ 933 8186 🕐 Mon, Wed–Sat 10–6 🚇 Atwater

LA BRIOCHE LYONNAISE (£)
The best pâtisserie in a city known for its cakes and confectioners. The chocolates and ice cream are sensational.
✚ F6 ✉ 1593 rue Saint-Denis between boulevard de Maisonnneuve and rue Emery ☎ 842 7017 🕐 Daily breakfast, lunch, dinner 🚇 Berri-UQAM

CAFÉ CYKLAMEN (£)
An art gallery in Vieux-Montréal that serves muffins, croissants, raw-milk cheeses and homemade jams.
✚ G7 ✉ 370 Place Royale ☎ 842 9861 🕐 Thu–Sat 9–9; Sun–Wed 9–6 🚇 Place d'Armes

LES GÂTERIES CAFÉ (£)
A favourite among writers and artists. The house coffee is a blend of 40 kinds of beans.
✚ F6 ✉ 3443 rue Saint-Denis ☎ 843 6235 🕐 Daily breakfast, lunch, dinner 🚇 Sherbrooke

CAFÉ GRANO (£)
Deliberately seedy and singularly ungracious, but the sandwiches – combos like smoked chicken, bocconcini, pesto and tomatoes – are superb.
✚ F6 ✉ 3647 boulevard Saint-Laurent ☎ 840 9000 🕐 Daily from noon 🚇 Saint-Laurent 🚌 51

CAFÉ SANTROPOL (£)
Charming student and alternative café with largely vegetarian food, over 60 herbal teas, many ice creams, malts and sodas, and plenty of fruit juices, salads and quiches.
✚ E6 ✉ 3990 rue Saint-Urbain ☎ 842 3110 🕐 Tue–Fri lunch, dinner; Sat dinner; Sun brunch, dinner 🚇 Sherbrooke

CAFÉ TOMAN (£)
Sedate Czech city centre pâtisserie. Great cakes, chocolates, salads, soups and sandwiches.
✚ E8 ✉ 1421 rue Mackay ☎ 844 1605 🕐 Thu, Fri 10–7; Tue, Wed, Sat 10–6. Closed for 4 weeks in the summer 🚇 Guy-Concordia

On the pavement
Good coffee and reasonably priced snacks are available in just about any pavement café. Find a busy one, pick a sunny table and sit for as long as you want watching the world go by. The 50 or so cafés in the A L Van Houtte chain, a company that started life as a coffee importer in 1919, are very reliable. Other good locally owned chains are the Brulerie Saint-Denis and the Café Dépôt. The Toronto-based Second Cup is making serious inroads, sprouting up all over the place like mushrooms after a rainstorm. No sign yet of the US giant Starbucks', though.

ART & ANTIQUES

Where to look

Antiques collectors with bulging wallets search for treasures in the lavish shops along rue Sherbrooke Ouest and in exclusive Westmount. The more modest crowd look on trendy Antique Alley on rue Notre-Dame Ouest. Real hunters haunt the shops on rue Amherst, where they can buy wooden toys in Antiquités Curiosités at No. 1769, or scavenge chrome fittings from the 1950s in Cité Déco at No. 1761.

L'ANTIQUAIRE JOYAL

Rosaries, crucifixes, religious art and other relics of early Québec plus two floors of Victorian furniture.

✚ G5 ✉ 1475 rue Amherst ☎ 524 0057 🚇 Beaudry

ANTIQUITÉS PHYLLIS FRIEDMAN

Classy city-centre shop with an excellent choice of high-quality antique English furniture and decorative accessories – Anglo-Irish glass, ceramics and crystal.

✚ E8 ✉ 1776 rue Sherbrooke Ouest ☎ 935 1991 🕐 Mon–Fri 10:30–6; Sat 10:30–5 🚇 Guy Métro

LE CHARIOT

The country's largest gallery devoted to Inuit art, one of the most distinctive and purely Canadian of souvenirs.

✚ G7 ✉ 446 place Jacques-Cartier ☎ 875 4995 🚌 38 🚇 Champ-de-Mars

COACH HOUSE ANTIQUES

China, silver, fine art, jewellery and furniture.

✚ D9 ✉ 135 avenue Greene ☎ 937 6191 🕐 Mon–Fri 9:30–5:30; Sat 10–4:30 🚇 Atwater

GUILDE CANADIENNE DES MÉTIERS D'ART

Canadian crafts such as blown glass, porcelain, pewter, tapestry and jewellery, plus a permanent exhibition of Inuit, First Peoples and other Canadian sculpture, prints and artefacts.

✚ E7 ✉ 2025 rue Peel ☎ 849 6091 🕐 Tue–Fri 9:30–6; Sat 10–5 🚇 Peel

HENRIETTA ANTONY

Large shop spread over four floors, with fine, often extremely old pieces, including good early Québécois furniture.

✚ D9 ✉ 4192 rue Sainte-Catherine Ouest at avenue Greene ☎ 935 9116 🕐 Tue–Fri 10–5:30; Sat 10–3 🚇 Atwater

LE VILLAGE DES ANTIQUAIRES

Fourteen dealers share this shop – specialists in furniture, jewellery, books and vintage clothing.

✚ E9 ✉ 1708 rue Notre-Dame Ouest ☎ 931 5121 🕐 Daily 11–5 🚇 Lionel-Groulx

LUCIE FAVREAU SPORTS MEMORABILIA

Just the place to pick up a hockey stick auto-graphed by a 1950s great or a 1940s football poster.

✚ E9 ✉ 1904 rue Notre-Dame Ouest ☎ 989 5117 🕐 Mon–Fri 10–6; Sat 10–5 🚇 Lionel-Groulx

PARENT MOQUIN ANTIQUITÉS

Lots of small sterling, silver plate and fine china.

✚ F9 ✉ 1650 rue Notre-Dame Ouest near rue Richmond ☎ 933 9435 🕐 Mon–Fri 11–6; Sat 11–5; Sun noon–5 🚇 Lucien l'Allier

PETIT MUSÉE

Sensational antiques from around the world, at stratospheric prices. Worth a visit even if you don't intend to buy.

✚ E8 ✉ 1494 rue Sherbrooke Ouest ☎ 937 6161 🕐 Tue–Sat 10–5 🚇 Guy-Concordia

BOOKS & NEWSPAPERS

BIBLIOMANIA BOOK SHOPPE
One of the best second-hand shops in the city with titles in French and English, and the occasional rarity.
✚ D6 ✉ 1841 Sainte-Catherine Ouest ☎ 933 8156 ⏱ Mon–Fri 11:30–6:30; Sat 11–6; Sun 12:30–2 Ⓜ Guy-Concordia
🚌 15

CHAPTERS
The city's largest stock of English-language titles.
✚ E8 ✉ 1171 rue Sainte-Catherine Ouest at rue Stanley ☎ 849 8825 ⏱ Daily 9AM–11PM Ⓜ Peel

DOUBLE HOOK CANADIAN BOOKS
Canadian literature and children's books in a charming Victorian house in Westmount.
✚ D9 ✉ 1235 avenue Greene at rue Sainte-Catherine Ouest ☎ 932 5093 ⏱ Mon–Wed 9:30–5:30; Thu, Fri 9:30–8; Sat 9:30–5 Ⓜ Atwater

EX LIBRIS
This elegant grey-stone building on rue Sherbrooke houses a fine collection of secondhand books.
✚ E8 ✉ 1628b Sherbrooke Ouest ☎ 932 1689 ⏱ Mon–Thu 11–6; Fri 11–8; Sat 11–5 Ⓜ Guy-Concordia

INDIGO
This bright, airy branch of a Toronto-based chain, in Place Montréal Trust, has a café and a selection of books that rivals Chapters.
✚ F7 ✉ 1500 avenue McGill ☎ 281 5549 ⏱ Daily 9AM–11PM Ⓜ McGill

LIBRAIRIE RENAUD-BRAY
Predominantly French-language chain for books, CDs, magazines and stationery.
✚ B8 ✉ 5252 Côtes-des-Neiges ☎ 342 1515 ⏱ Daily 8AM–midnight Ⓜ Côte-des-Neiges

NICHOLAS HOARE BOOKS
Specialises in British titles, 'beaux-livres', and classical and jazz CDs.
✚ D9 ✉ 1366 avenue Greene ☎ 933 4201 ⏱ Mon–Wed 9:30–6; Thu, Fri 9:30–9; Sat 9–5; Sun noon–5 Ⓜ Atwater

PARAGRAPHE BOOK STORE
Popular with serious book lovers and students. Lectures and readings by leading Canadian authors.
✚ E7 ✉ 2220 avenue McGill-College ☎ 845 5811 ⏱ Mon–Fri 7AM–11PM; Sat, Sun 9AM–11PM Ⓜ McGilll

ULYSSES LA LIBRAIRIE DU VOYAGE
Travel books and guides in French and English as well as maps and assorted travel-related artefacts. Several branches.
✚ F7 ✉ 560 avenue du Président-Kennedy near avenue Union ☎ 843 7222 ⏱ Mon–Wed 10–6; Thu, Fri 10–8; Sat 10–5; Sun noon–5 Ⓜ McGill
✚ E5 ✉ 4176 rue Saint-Denis ☎ 843 9447 ⏱ Mon–Fri 9:30–9; Sat 9:30–6; Sun 11–6 Ⓜ Mont-Royal

UNIVERSITÉ MCGILL
Well-stocked and intelligent.
✚ E7 ✉ 3420 McTavish ☎ 398 7444 ⏱ Mon–Sat 8:30AM–10PM Ⓜ Peel

Global press
For foreign newspapers try:
Metropolitan News
✉ 1109 rue Cypress at the corner of Peel, near Square-Dorchester ☎ 866 9227
Multimags
✉ 1570 boulevard de Maisonneuve Ouest, near rue Mackay ☎ 935 7044
Maison de la Presse Internationale
✉ 728 rue Sainte-Catherine Ouest ☎ 954 0333

MEN'S & WOMEN'S CLOTHES

Taxes

Federal and provincial taxes on most purchases total a little over 15 per cent. You can reclaim this on purchases of $100 and over (➤ 90).

Rue Chabanel

The heart and soul of Canada's garment industry is compressed into an eight-block stretch of this street in Montréal's north end. And every Saturday from about 8:30 to 1, the area's dozens of tiny factories and importers open to the public. Bargains abound and prices often 'include taxes' if you pay cash. Start at boulevard Saint-Laurent and work your way west.

ARTEFACT

Charming shop in trendy Saint-Denis that specialises in minimalist Québec designs for women.
E5 ⊠ 4117 Saint-Denis ☎ 842 2780 Mon–Fri noon–6; Sat 11–5; Sun noon–5 Mont-Royal 50

BRISSON ET BRISSON

The most exclusive men's clothing store in Montréal with a wide selection of hand-crafted shoes and clothes by big-name designers.
E8 ⊠ 1472 rue Sherbrooke Ouest ☎ 937 7456 Mon–Fri 9–6; Sat 9–5 Guy-Concordia

LA CACHE

The premier store of a chain covering Canada selling pretty store-label clothes, linens and gifts.
D9 ⊠ 1353 avenue Greene near rue Sherbrooke Ouest ☎ 935 4361 Mon–Wed 9:30–6; Thu, Fri 9:30–7; Sat 9:30–5; Sun noon–5 Atwater

LE CHÂTEAU

Canada-wide chain specialising in contemporary high fashion seconds at very low prices.
E8 ⊠ 1310 rue Sainte-Catherine Ouest at rue de la Montagne ☎ 866 2481 Mon–Fri 10–6; Sat 10–5; Sun noon–5 Peel

CHAS JOHNSON & SONS

This fine traditional tailor's shop with three kilt makers on call is one of the few places in Canada still offering made-to-measure Highland regalia. It also stocks the necessary Scottish accessories – hose, sporrans, jackets, skean dhus – as well as a full line of men's wear.
F7 ⊠ 1184 place Philippe (near boulevard René-Lévesque) ☎ 878 1931 Tue–Fri 9–5:30; Sat 9:30–4:30 McGill

GIORGIO

Two chic stores offer top names in men's and women's high fashion.
E7 ⊠ Giorgio Femme (women): Le Cours Mont-Royal, 1455 rue Peel ☎ 282 0294 ⊠ Giorgio Montréal (men): Maison Alcan 1176 rue Sherbrooke Ouest ☎ 287 1928 Mon–Wed 9:30–6; Thu, Fri 9:30–9; Sat 9:30–5:30 Peel

PIERRE, JEAN, JACQUES

Dressy and casual clothes for men, with an emphasis on Canadian design.
D5 ⊠ 150 avenue Laurier Ouest ☎ 270 8392 Laurier 51

L'UOMO

Top designer menswear plus John Lobb and Fratelli Rossetti shoes.
F7 ⊠ 1452 rue Peel at Sainte-Catherine Ouest ☎ 844 1008 Mon–Wed 9–6; Thu, Fri 9AM–9PM; Sat 9–5:30 Peel

SCARLETT O'HARA

Ultra-trendy shop with its own line of daring women's fashions.
E5 ⊠ 254 avenue Mont-Royal Est ☎ 844 9435 Mon–Wed 11–6; Thu, Fri 11–9; Sat 11–5 Mont-Royal

ACCESSORIES & FINE JEWELLERY

BIRKS

One of the country's most prestigious and longest-established jewellers, particularly known for its silverware and distinctive blue packaging. You'll also find high-quality china and crystal. Of the several city locations, this branch is particularly worth a visit just for a look at its wonderfully striking art deco interior.

✚ F7 ✉ 1240 Square-Phillips ☎ 397 2511 🕐 Mon–Wed 10–6; Thu, Fri 10–9; Sat 9:30–5; Sun noon–5 🚇 McGill

BROWN CHAUSSURES

Fashionable and expensive men's and women's shoes, boots and bags. This popular chain has half a dozen branches around the city.

✚ F7 ✉ 1 place Ville-Marie, rue University ☎ 861 8925 🕐 Mon–Wed 9–6; Thu, Fri 9–9; Sat 9–5; Sun noon–5 🚇 McGill, Bonaventure

CHAPOFOLIE

Both men and women can complete their fashion purchases here, at the largest hat store in the city.

✚ E5 ✉ 3944 rue Saint-Denis ☎ 982 0036 🕐 Tue–Fri noon–6; Sat 11–6; Sun 1–6 🚇 Mont-Royal

HEMSLEYS

Montréal's oldest jewellers; like Birks they also sell silverware and china although not as wide a range.

✚ F7 ✉ 660 rue Sainte-Catherine Ouest ☎ 866 3706 🕐 Mon–Wed 10–6; Thu, Fri 10–9; Sat noon–5 🚇 McGill

HENRI HENRI

Men with a sense of style have been buying their Borsalinos and Stetsons from this east-end haberdashery since 1932.

✚ F6 ✉ 189 rue Sainte-Catherine Est ☎ 288 0109 🕐 Mon–Thu 9–6; Fri 9–9; Sat 9–5 🚇 Saint-Laurent

KARLS CHAUSSURES

This delightfully cluttered store, in business since 1934, stocks shoes, boots, trainers and hiking wear from Timberland, Adidas, Doc Marten, Converse, Birkenstock and other major brands.

✚ E5 ✉ 4259 boulevard Saint-Laurent near rue Rachel ☎ 849 3839 🚇 Mont-Royal 🚌 29, 55

KAUFMANN DE SUISSE

Crafts its own line of exclusive jewellery.

✚ E8 ✉ 2195 rue Crescent ☎ 848 0595 🕐 Mon–Fri 9–6; Sat 10–5 🚇 Guy-Concordia

SOXBOX ACCESSORIES

Come to this spot slightly south of the central area if you are desperate to find exactly the right socks, stockings or tights. Top European and North American manufacturers are represented.

✚ D9 ✉ 1357 avenue Greene at the corner of rue Sherbrooke Ouest ☎ 931 4980 🕐 Mon–Fri 9–6; Sat 9–5 🚇 Atwater

Furs

Montréal owes its early commercial success to the fur trade, and trends away from the wearing of furs notwithstanding, the city still boasts some of Canada's best furriers.

Grosvenor-McComber (✉ 400 boulevard de Maisonneuve Ouest ☎ 288 1255) has been in business since 1895. Birger Christensen at Holt Renfrew (✉ 1300 rue Sherbrooke Ouest ☎ 842 5111) is a favourite among the city's elite.

GIFTS

Sweet and musical

Looking for something 'typical' to take home? For something sweet, think maple. Québec produces more than two thirds of the world's supply of maple syrup so, not surprisingly, the stuff is ubiquitous on Montréal breakfast tables, and sweets, toffee, butter and sugar made from maple sap are common treats. A good time to buy is in spring when the supply is plentiful. Best prices are at farmers' markets.

For something more lasting, consider music. Because of its linguistic isolation, Québec has produced a rich popular culture of its own that's better-known in France than in the US or even the rest of Canada. Try Archambault (see main entry this page) for the latest hits, or look for recordings by singers Gilles Vigneault and Félix Leclerc or seminal rock musician Robert Charlebois.

ARCHAMBAULT

Montréal's own music shop is excellent for current releases, classical music and Québec pops. It also has an extensive selection of song books and sheet music.
✚ F5 ✉ 175 rue Sainte-Catherine Est ☎ 281 0367 ◷ Mon–Wed 9:30–8; Thu, Fri 9:30–9; Sat, Sun 11–5 ⊜ Berri-UQAM

CANADIENS BOUTIQUE

Posters, pucks, jerseys, and other memorabilia all bearing the famous team emblem.
✚ F8 ✉ Molson Centre, 1250 rue de la Gauchetière ☎ 989 2836 ◷ Mon–Wed 9:30–6; Thu, Fri 9:30–9; Sat 9:30–5 ⊜ Bonaventure

DAVIDOFF TABAC

Top-quality cigars from around the world, as well as pipes, clippers, hardwood cigar boxes and other smoking paraphernalia.
✚ E7 ✉ 1452 rue Sherbrooke Ouest ☎ 289 9118 ◷ Mon–Wed 10–6; Thu, Fri 10–9; Sat 10–6; Sun 11–4 ⊜ Guy

EDIFICE BELAGO

This nondescript city centre building is essentially a mall for art galleries, showing established and upcoming artists. Some of the best include (on the fifth floor) Troise Pointes and Optica Centre for Contemporary Art.
✚ F7 ✉ 372 rue Sainte-Catherine Ouest ☎ Troise Pointes 866 8008; Optica 874 1666 ◷ Tue–Fri 10–5; Sat noon–5 ⊜ Place-des-Arts

HMV

Airy, comprehensive and well-organised; the best place for CDs and tapes.
✚ F7 ✉ 1010 rue Sainte-Catherine Ouest ☎ 875 0765 ◷ Mon–Fri 9:30–9; Sat 9–5; Sun 10–5 ⊜ Peel

KANUK

Parkas, overcoats, fleece wear, gloves, socks and everything else needed to survive when the mercury hits the bottom of the thermometer.
✚ E5 ✉ 485 rue Rachel Est ☎ 284 4494 ◷ Mon–Wed 9–6; Thu, Fri 9–9; Sat 9:30–5; Sun 11–5 ⊜ Mont-Royal ⊟ 30

LINEN CHEST

Simply the best for bedding, towels, kitchen linen and the like.
✚ F7 ✉ Promenades de la Cathédrale, 625 rue Sainte-Catherine Ouest ☎ 282 9525 ◷ Mon–Wed 10–6; Thu, Fri 10–9; Sat 10–5; Sun noon–5 ⊜ McGill

LA MAISON DU STYLO PEEL

Lovely pens and pencils.
✚ F7 ✉ 1212 avenue Union ☎ 866 1340 ◷ Mon–Fri 8–6; Sat 10–4 ⊜ McGill

MDI MULTI DESIGN INTERNATIONAL

Funky place for unusual gadgets for the home.
✚ D5 ✉ 274 avenue Laurier Ouest ☎ 277 0052 ◷ Mon–Wed 10–6; Thu, Fri 10–9; Sat, Sun 10–5 ⊜ Laurier ⊟ 51

OINKOINK

Toys and fashion for young children.
✚ D10 ✉ 1234 avenue Greene ☎ 939 2634 ◷ Mon–Fri 9:30–6; Sat 9:30–5 ⊜ Atwater

MARKETS

LE FAUBOURG SAINTE-CATHERINE

The Faubourg complex is easily accessible from the city centre. Clothing and craft outlets compete with food, fruit and vegetable stalls over three levels while inexpensive cafés and food kiosks surround a central atrium.

➕ E7 ✉ rue Guy at rue Sainte-Catherine Ouest ☎ 939 3663 🕐 Daily 9AM–9:30PM 🚇 Guy-Concordia

MARCHÉ ATWATER

This outlying market is known for meat and vegetables and other specialist foods. It is close to a Métro station and near the Lachine Canal towpath. It's also a great place to buy delicious maple syrup.

➕ E10 ✉ avenue Atwater south of rue Notre-Dame Ouest ☎ 937 7754 🕐 Thu–Fri 8AM–9PM; Sat 8–6; Sun 8–5; Mon–Wed 8–6 🚇 Lionel-Groulx

MARCHÉ ST-JACQUES

Within walking distance of the Quartier Latin and devoted to plants and flowers, this market is pretty enough to visit for its own sake.

➕ F5 ✉ rue Ontario Est at rue Amherst ☎ 937 7754 🕐 May–Oct: Thu, Fri 7AM–9PM; Sat, Sun 7–5; Mon–Wed 7–6 🚇 Sherbrooke, Beaudry

MARCHÉ JEAN-TALON

Montréal's largest public market lies some distance from the city centre, but is just 5 minutes' walk from two Métro stations and lies at the heart of Montréal's Little Italy.

➕ B3–B4 ✉ rue Jean-Talon Est between avenues Henri-Julien and Casgrain ☎ 277 1588 🕐 Thu, Fri 8AM–9PM; Sat 8–6; Sun 8–5; Mon–Wed 8–6 🚇 Jean-Talon, De Castelnau

MARCHÉ LACHINE

The location of this small farmers' market near the end of the lovely Lachine Canal bicycle trail makes it a delightful place to stop for picnic fare.

➕ Off map at A13 ✉ Corner of 17ième avenue and rue Piché in Lachine 🕐 Thu, Fri 7AM–9PM; Sat 7–5; Mon–Wed 7–6

MARCHÉ DE L'OUEST

One of the island's most popular markets is deep in the West Island suburbs. Look for quality butchers, fishmongers, bulk spice shops, bakeries, pâtisseries and specialist food boutiques. From early summer to late autumn, farmers sell flowers, vegetables, berries, honey and maple products outdoors.

➕ Off map at A13 ✉ 11, 600 de Salaberry, Dollard-des-Armeaux ☎ 685 0119 🕐 Sat–Wed 9–6; Thu, Fri 9–9

MARCHÉ MAISONNEUVE

Stop at this fruit and vegetable market in a vintage building near Parc Olympique when you're in the area.

➕ H1–H2 ✉ rue Ontario Est at boulevard Morgan ☎ 253 3993 🕐 Thu, Fri 8AM–9PM; Sat 8–6; Sun 8–5; Mon–Wed 8–6 🚇 Pie-XI

Fleas move out

The Vieux-Port closed the only flea market of any size within Montréal's city limits several years ago to make way for the city's science centre. But there are several good-sized markets on the city perimeter. The best by far is Finnegans (➕ off map at A13 ✉ 700 Main Road, Hudson ☎ 450/458 4377 🕐 May–Oct: Sat), which has been operating for 26 years in a barn and an adjoining field on the outskirts of town in the semi-rural hamlet of Hudson. While not the region's biggest market, its merchandise is several notches above the norm. At least 100 merchants and dealers sell clocks, silverware, dishes, glassware, wood-carvings of herons and roosters, wrought-iron goods, plants, furniture, dried flowers, honey, lampshades, jewellery, handsome wooden toys and bric à brac. Many Montréalers make a day out of an excursion, stopping for lunch or dinner at the Willow Inn (✉ 208 Maid Road ☎ 450/458 7006).

75

MALLS & DEPARTMENT STORES

Mall shopping

The great advantage of shopping in Montreal's state-of-the-art malls, of course, is that it's an all-season endeavour – an important consideration in a city with cruel winters and hot, humid summers. Most of them are linked into the Underground City's (► 34) extensive network of tunnels and Métro lines. Many of the city's major department stores are also connected to the system, and some of them – notably upmarket competitors Ogilvy (► 77) and Holt Renfrew (see main entry this page) – have become mini-malls, opening shops within shops to showcase such designers as Jean-Claude Chacok, Guy Laroche, Lily Simon and Cacherel.

LE CENTRE EATON

Ironically, the venerable Canadian department store that gave this mall its name closed its doors in 1999. But the mall – the largest in the central core with five floors of boutiques and shops – is still thriving.

✚ F7 ✉ 705 rue Sainte-Catherine Ouest ☎ 288 3708 🕐 Mon–Fri 10–9; Sat 10–5; Sun noon–5 🚇 McGill

COMPLEXE DESJARDINS

This vast multi-tiered complex, one of the largest malls in the east of the centre, belongs to the powerful Mouvement Desjardins conglomerate. In addition to about 100 shops you'll find restaurants and bistros, walk-in dental and medical facilities, cinemas, offices and a large piazza used for cultural events. Fountains and exotic plants make the place unusually pleasurable.

✚ F7 ✉ rue Sainte-Catherine Ouest at Saint-Urbain ☎ 281 1870 🕐 Mon–Wed 9:30–6; Thu, Fri 9:30–9; Sat 9:30–5; Sun noon–5 🚇 Place-des-Arts

LES COURS MONT-ROYAL

This elegant shopping centre is in the old Mount Royal Hotel, a jazz-age palace that was the largest hotel in the British Empire when it opened in 1922 with 1,100 rooms. When developers gutted the place in 1987, they left the exterior intact and saved part of the old lobby with a crystal chandelier that used to illuminate the Monte Carlo Casino. The inner court rises 10 storeys to the roof, and is surrounded by balconies and fashionable shops.

✚ E7 ✉ 1550 rue Metcalfe 🚇 Peel

HOLT RENFREW

Established in 1837, this is the oldest of the city's large stores, and has occupied its present distinctive six-storey home since 1936. It is particularly known for its furs, and has supplied four generations of British royalty (among others), but also sells other quality goods and fashions.

✚ E7 ✉ 1300 rue Sherbrooke Ouest at rue de la Montagne ☎ 842 5111 🕐 Mon–Wed 10–6; Thu, Fri 10–9; Sat 10–6; Sun 11:30–5 🚇 Peel

LA BAIE (THE BAY)

Construction of the establishment now known as La Baie in 1890 proved the catalyst for most of the subsequent retail development on rue Sainte-Catherine, Montréal's main shopping street. La Baie, successor to the venerable Hudson's Bay Company, emphasises not only clothes but also other good, mid-range items, the most famous being the trademark Hudson's Bay coats and blankets.

✚ F7 ✉ 585 rue Sainte-Catherine Ouest ☎ 281 4422 🕐 Mon–Fri 9:30–7; Sat 8AM–9PM; Sun 10–5 🚇 McGill

SOCIÉTÉ DE MUSIQUE CONTEMPORAINE DE QUÉBEC (SMCQ)

A well-established modern classical ensemble.
☎ 843 9305

I MUSICI

A much-lauded chamber ensemble.
☎ 982 6037

LE STUDIO DE MUSIQUE ANCIENNE,

An early music society.
☎ 861 2626

McGILL CHAMBER ORCHESTRA

Performs at the Place des Arts and another key classical venue, the Pollack Hall.
🚩 F7 ✉ 555 rue Sherbrooke Ouest ☎ 398 4547 🚇 McGill

DANCE

Most of Montréal's major dance troupes perform at the Place des Arts and neighbourhood cultural centres (Maisons de Culture).
❓ See press (▶ 79) for details

BALLETS CLASSIQUES DE MONTRÉAL

Established in 1964; the city's most famous traditional ballet company.
☎ 866 1771

LES GRANDS BALLETS CANADIENS

Québec's leading traditional ballet troupe.
☎ 849 8681

LALALA HUMAN STEPS

An internationally acclaimed avant-garde dance company.
☎ 277 9090

LES BALLETS JAZZ DE MONTRÉAL

Highly regarded modern dance troupe.
☎ 982 6771

FESTIVAL INTERNATIONAL DE NOUVELLE DANSE

For two weeks in late September and early October of odd-numbered years, the city hosts this popular modern dance festival.
☎ 287 1423

OPERA

L'OPÉRA DE MONTRÉAL

Founded in 1979, the city's opera company stages four productions every year at the Place des Arts.
☎ 985 2258

THEATRE

THÉÂTRE DU RIDEAU VERT

One of the best-known of the French-language theatres in Montréal.
🚩 D4 ✉ 4664 rue St-Denis, ☎ 844 1793 🚇 Laurier

CENTAUR THEATRE

The city's foremost English-language theatre.
🚩 G7 ✉ 453 rue St-François-Xavier ☎ 288 3161 🚇 Place d'Armes

COMEDY

COMEDY NEST

Venue for local and visiting comics.
🚩 G7 ✉ 1740b boulevard René-Lévesque Ouest ☎ 931 8841 🚇 Guy-Concordia

Place des Arts

Montréal's showcase for the performing arts has five major performance spaces including the 2,982-seat Salle Wilfrid-Pelletier concert hall. The Place des Arts houses the Orchestre Symphonique de Montréal, the Opéra de Montréal and the city's principal ballet troupe, Les Grands Ballets Canadiens. Chamber music, plays, other concerts and an informal Sunday-morning breakfast concert series known as Sons et Brioches are also held here.

🚩 F7 ✉ 260, boulevard de Maisonneuve Ouest

☎ Information 285 4200; tickets 842 2112

🕐 Box office Mon–Fri 10–6

🚇 Place-des-Arts

LIVE MUSIC VENUES

More live music

Salsathèque (➤ 79) has pulsating Latin rhythms with dancing to match; and Pub le Vieux Dublin (➤ 78) offers live Celtic music that strikes a chord with visitors and Montréalers alike.

L'AIR DU TEMPS

Small, smoky and intimate; this archetypal jazz club with a great old-fashioned interior lies at the heart of Vieux-Montréal. Come early for a decent seat.

🛉 G8 ✉ 191 rue St-Paul Ouest ☎ 842 2003 🕐 Live music Wed–Sun 8:30PM–3AM 🚇 Square-Victoria 💵 Cover charge

AUX DEUX PIERROTS

A crowded and convivial Vieux-Montréal venue devoted to traditional Québécois folk-music. Performances are on the terrace when the weather warms up.

🛉 G7 ✉ 104 rue St-Paul Ouest at rue St-Sulpice ☎ 861 1270 🕐 Mon–Fri 9AM–6PM 🚇 Place-d'Armes

BIDDLES

Jazz musician Charlie Biddles is the heart and soul of this city-centre local. Plus some pretty fine chicken and ribs.

🛉 F7 ✉ 2060 rue Aylmer near rue de Maisonneuve Ouest ☎ 842 8656 🕐 Mon–Fri 11:30AM–1AM; Sat 5PM–2:30AM; Sun 6PM–1AM. Live jazz every night 🚇 McGill 💵 Cover charge on weekends and for major acts ❓ Booking recommended

CAFÉ CAMPUS

This small venue has a reputation for show-casing great indie bands; popular with English- and French-speaking kids alike. DJs strike up and the dance-floor fills once the bands go.

🛉 F6 ✉ 57 rue Prince-Arthur Est ☎ 844 3430 🕐 Daily 1PM–4:30AM 🚇 Sherbrooke

HURLEY'S IRISH PUB

Montréal's Celtic music craze started in this comfortable two-floor city centre club – and it is still a favourite with the city's Irish community.

🛉 E8 ✉ 1225 rue Crescent ☎ 861 4111 🕐 Daily noon–3AM 🚇 Peel, Guy-Concordia

LE CLUB SODA

Hosts live music as well as stand-up comedy and other shows. It buzzes during the Jazz and Juste Pour Rire festivals.

🛉 D5 ✉ 5240 avenue du Parc ☎ 270 7848 🕐 Daily 8PM–3AM 🚇 Laurier 🚌 80, 535

LES BEAUX ESPRITS

Jazz and blues are the staples at this popular and intimate club on the vibrant rue St-Denis.

🛉 F5 ✉ 2073 rue St-Denis ☎ 844 0882 🚇 Sherbrooke

QUAI DES BRUMES

Two quite different jazz bars share a building on rue St-Denis (albeit with separate entrances). Downstairs is the calm and intimate Quai des Brumes. Upstairs is the bigger and louder Le Central which draws a college-age crowd.

🛉 E5 ✉ 4479 rue St-Denis ☎ 845 9010 🕐 Daily 3PM–3AM 🚇 Mont-Royal

PUB CHEZ NANIGANS

Reads Shenanigans without violating Quebec's French-only sign rules; also a good place to hear bands from Canada's east coast.

🛉 G7 ✉ 43 rue St-Jacques ☎ 288 0990 🕐 Daily Tue–Sat 🚇 Place d'Armes

SPORT

BASEBALL

The Expos play in the Olympic Stadium from April to September.
✚ G1 ✉ Stade Olympique, 4549 avenue Pierre-de-Coubertin ☎ Information 253 3434; tickets 846 3976 Ⓜ Viau

CYCLING

Montréal has over 20 specialised cycle path. Rent bikes from:
Vélo Aventure ✉ Quai King-Edward ☎ 847 0666
Accès Oble ✉ Place Jacques-Cartier ☎ 525 8888
Bicycletterie JR, ✉ 151 rue Rachel Est ☎ 843 6989

GOLF

Golf Le Village ✚ G1 ✉ rue Sherbrooke/rue Viau ☎ 872 4653 Ⓜ Viau
Club de Golf Deux-Montagnes offers 36 championship holes on a beautiful, lakeside course ✚ Off map at A13 ☎ 450/472 4653
Club de Gold Mont-Gabriel This panoramic course is an hour's drive from Montréal in the Laurentians ✚ Off map at A13 ☎ 800/668 5253

FOOTBALL

The Alouettes of the professional Canadian Football League play on real grass at the open-air Molson Stadium on the McGill University campus ✚ E7 ☎ 254 2400

HOCKEY

Montréal's much-loved hockey team, Les Canadiens, plays at the Molson Centre between October and mid-June.
✚ F8 ✉ Molson Centre, 1260 rue de la Gauchetière Ouest Ⓜ Bonaventure

JOGGING

Parc Angrignon offers gentle, scenic cinder trails or puff up Mont-Royal on trails of varying steepness.

MOTOR RACING

The Formula One Grand Prix takes place every June on the Île Notre-Dame.
✚ J5–K8 ✉ Circuit Gilles-Villeneuve ☎ 871 1421 Ⓜ Île Ste-Hélène

SQUASH

Book court time at the Nautilus Centre St-Laurent Côte-de-Liesse Racquet Club.
✚ Off map at A8 ✉ 8305 chemin Côte-de-Liesse ☎ 739 3654 Ⓜ Du Collège

SWIMMING

Olympic Park has *six* Olympic-sized pools
✚ G1 ✉ Parc olympique, 4141 avenue Pierre-de-Coubertin ☎ 252 4622 or 252 8687 Ⓜ Viau. There are also three outdoor pools on the Île Sainte-Hélène and a city-run beach on the Île Notre-Dame
✚ H4–K8 ☎ 872 6211 Ⓜ Île Ste-Hélène.

WINDSURFING AND SAILING

Small boats and boards can be rented from:
Société de l'Île Notre-Dame ✉ Île Notre-Dame ☎ 872 6903 and at the nearby town of Lachine from:
L'École de Voile de Lachine ✉ 2015 boulevard St-Joseph, Lachine ☎ 634 4326

City passion

The Canadiens team has won the National Hockey League's championship Stanley Cup a record 24 times since 1929, which is why they are sometimes called Les Glorieux. No city in Canada is more passionate about Canada's unofficial national sport than Montréal and no uniform is more familiar to hockey fans than the red and white jersey of the Montréal Canadiens with its famous but obscure CH motif. There was a myth the letters stood for Habitants Canadiens, which is why the club is sometimes referred to affectionately as 'the Hab', but the letters, in fact, stand for Club de Hockey Canadien.

LUXURY HOTELS

Prices and location

Depending on the season, expect to pay to $145 to $250 per night for a double room in Montréal's luxury hotels. City centre hotels come in all categories, while budget properties cluster around the Voyageur bus terminal and St-Denis. At all price levels, many hotels offer cheaper off-season rates, two-night and weekend breaks, and 'family plan' deals, where children can stay free with two adults. Some provide a third bed in a double room for a modest charge. Apartment hotels rent rooms by the day and may have small kitchens.

BONAVENTURE HILTON INTERNATIONAL

Astride the Place Bonaventure mall and exhibition centre. Swimming pool and extensive gardens.

✚ F8 ✉ 1 place Bonaventure ☎ 878 2332 or toll-free 1 800/445 8667 in Canada, 800 HILTONS in the US 🚇 Bonaventure

CENTRE SHERATON

Luxurious convention hotel in town. Huge foyer full of greenery.

✚ F7 ✉ 201 boulevard René-Lévesque Ouest ☎ 878 2000 🚇 Place-des-Arts

DELTA MONTRÉAL

Large rooms, most with balconies; pool and fitness facilities. Vast foyer.

✚ F7 ✉ 475 avenue du President-Kennedy ☎ 286 1986 or 877/286 1986 🚇 Place-des-Arts

HÔTEL LE GERMAIN

Once dowdy city-centre office building has been transformed into a sleek boutique hotel.

✚ E7 ✉ 2050 rue Mansfield ☎ 849 2050 or 800/463 5253 🚇 McGill

LOEWS HÔTEL VOGUE

Bathrooms all have whirlpool baths, televisions and phones in this fashionable city-centre hotel.

✚ E8 ✉ 1425 rue de la Montagne ☎ 285 5555 or 800/465 6654 🚇 Peel/Guy-Concordia

HÔTEL INTERCONTINENTAL MONTRÉAL

24 storeys, with health club and pool.

✚ F7–G7 ✉ 360 rue St-Antoine Ouest ☎ 987 9900 or toll-free 1 800/361 3600 🚇 Square-Victoria

OMNI MONTRÉAL

Top-notch service, fine rooms, many with good views of Mont-Royal. Very good pavement-level restaurant, Opus II.

✚ E7 ✉ 1050 rue Sherbrooke Ouest ☎ 284 1110 or 800/843 6664

PIERRE DU CALVERT

Sumptuously decorated with antiques, this 18th-century inn is one of the city's oldest buildings.

✚ G8 ✉ 405 rue Bonsecours ☎ 282 1725 🚇 Champ-de-Mars

LA REINE ÉLIZABETH

A Canadian Pacific hotel atop the Gare Centrale, with modern comforts.

✚ F7 ✉ 900 boulevard René-Léveque Ouest ☎ 861 3511 or toll-free 1 800/441 1414 🚇 Bonaventure

RITZ CARLTON MONTRÉAL

Montreal's stateliest hotel – an Edwardian dream. Richard Burton and Liz Taylor celebrated their second wedding here.

✚ E7 ✉ 1228 rue Sherbrooke Ouest ☎ 842 4212 or 800/241 333 🚇 Peel

MARRIOTT CHÂTEAU CHAMPLAIN

In one of the city's most distinctive skyscrapers, with 600 rooms.

✚ F8 ✉ 1 place du Canada ☎ 878 9000 or toll-free 1 800/441 1414 🚇 Bonaventure

MID-RANGE HOTELS

AUBERGE BONAPARTE

Delightful 32-room inn in the heart of Vieux-Montréal has rare views of the Basilique Notre-Dame gardens next door.

➕ G7 ✉ 447 rue St-Françoise-Xavier ☎ 844 1448 🚇 Place d'Armes

AUBERGE DE LA FONTAINE

Intimate, with just 21 rooms. North of the centre and some distance from a Métro station.

➕ F4 ✉ 1301 rue Rachel Est ☎ 597 0166 or toll-free 1 800/597 0597 🚇 Mont-Royal

AUBERGE DU VIEUX-PORT

Rooms with brass beds and casement windows look over rue St-Paul or the Vieux-Port.

➕ G7 ✉ 97 rue de la Commune Est ☎ 876 0081 🚇 Place d'Armes

BEST WESTERN EUROPA CENTRE-VILLE

Good location but more expensive than some mid-range hotels.

➕ E8 ✉ 1240 rue Drummond ☎ 866 6492 or toll-free 1 800/361 3000 🚇 Peel

CHÂTEAU VERSAILLES

Charming and popular.

➕ E8 ✉ 1659 rue Sherbrooke Ouest ☎ 933 3611 or toll-free 1 800/361 7199 in Canada, 1 800/361 3664 in US 🚇 Guy-Concordia

HÔTEL DE L'INSTITUT

Top civil servants love this little hotel on the top floors of Québec's best hotel-training school right on Square St-Louis.

➕ F6 ✉ 3535 rue St-Denis ☎ 282 5120 or 800/361 5111 🚇 Sherbrooke

HÔTEL DE LA MONTAGNE

Spacious if a trifle bland rooms. Good restaurants, rooftop terrace and pool.

➕ E8 ✉ 1430 rue de la Montagne ☎ 288 5656 or toll-free 1 800/361 6262 🚇 Peel

L'APPARTEMENT-IN-MONTRÉAL

Well-priced studios with kitchenettes. Pool and terrace.

➕ F7 ✉ 455 rue Sherbrooke Ouest ☎ 284 3634 or toll-free 1 800/363 3010 🚇 Place-des-Arts, McGill

LE NOUVEL HÔTEL

Functional hotel with studio, two/three room apartments.

➕ E8 ✉ 1740 boulevard René-Lévesque Ouest ☎ 931 8841 or toll-free 1 800/363 6063 🚇 Guy-Concordia

LES PASSANTS DU SANS SOUCY

The first choice in Vieux-Montréal. All nine rooms have antique furniture and beamed ceilings.

➕ G7 ✉ 171 rue St-Paul Ouest ☎ 842 2634 🚇 Square-Victoria, Place d'Armes

DELTA CENTRE-VILLE

Convention favourite with stunning atrium, outstanding restaurants. Pool and health club.

➕ F7 ✉ 777 rue University ☎ 879 1370 or toll-free 800/268 1133 🚇 Square-Victoria

Booking

Although Greater Montréal has some 23,000 hotel beds, advance bookings are advisable, particularly between May and August. Even if you guarantee your booking with a credit card, reconfirm a few days ahead. Receptionists are usually bilingual in French and English. If you arrive without accommodation, the city's tourist offices will help you find a room (► 89).

BUDGET ACCOMMODATION

Bed and breakfast

Bed and breakfast options (*couette et café* in French) can be booked through tourist offices and through the following agencies:

Bed & Breakfast Downtown Network

✉ 3458 avenue Laval

☎ 289 9749 or toll-free 1 800/267 5180

Bed and Breakfast à Montréal Network

✉ 2033 rue St-Herbert

☎ 738 9410 or toll-free 1 800/738 4338

Chambre et petit déjeuners Bienvenue

✉ 3950 avenue Laval

☎ 844 5897 or toll-free 1 800/227 5897

HÔTEL LORD BERRI
Good modern hotel next to the Université du Québec á Montréal; convenient to St-Denis.
✚ G6 ✉ 1199 rue Berri
☎ 845 9236 or toll-free 800/363 0363 Ⓜ Berri-UQAM

HÔTEL AMERICAIN
Clean, eccentric city-centre hotel, near the Vieux-Port and Quartier-Latin. Rooms are in an older wing and a newer annexe where you'll also find suites with kitchenettes.
✚ G6 ✉ 1042 rue St-Denis
☎ 849 0616 Ⓜ Champ-de-Mars

HÔTEL LE ST-ANDRÉ
61 rooms close to Vieux-Montréal and St-Denis.
✚ G6 ✉ 1285 rue St-André
☎ 849 7070 or toll-free 1 800/265 7071 in Canada and the US Ⓜ Berri-UQAM

HÔTEL MANOIR SHERBROOKE
Converted Victorian building with pleasant rooms. Complimentary continental breakfast.
✚ F6 ✉ 157 rue Sherbrooke Est ☎ 845 0915/285 0895 or toll-free 1 800/203 5485 Ⓜ Sherbrooke

HÔTEL DE PARIS
Interesting old building with copper-roofed tower, convenient for rue Saint-Denis.
✚ F5 ✉ 901 rue Sherbrooke Est ☎ 522 6861 or toll-free 1 800/567 7217 Ⓜ Sherbrooke

LA RÉSIDENCE DU VOYAGEUR
There are 28 rooms, many with shared bath. Close to the centre and with complimentary continental breakfast.
✚ F5 ✉ 847 rue Sherbrooke Est ☎ 527 9515 Ⓜ Sherbrooke

MANOIR AMBROSE
With 22 rooms, these are some of the city centre's cheapest – you're just a couple of blocks from the centre. Rates include breakfast.
✚ E7–F8 ✉ 3422 rue Stanley ☎ 288 6922 Ⓜ Peel

YMCA/YWCA
Simple rooms for single, double and multiple occupancy. The Young Men's Christian Association has a women-only floor; the Young Women's Christian Association is for women only; men can use the facilities by day. Most YWCA rooms have shared bath and kitchen facilities available for guests.
✚ E7–E8 ✉ YMCA, 1450 rue Stanley ☎ 849 8393 Ⓜ Peel
✚ E–F8 ✉ YWCA, 1355 boulevard René-Lévesque Ouest ☎ 866 9941 ext. 505 or toll-free 1–800/400–YWCA Ⓜ Lucien-l'Allier

AUBERGE DE JEUNESSE-YOUTH HOSTEL
Superior hostel open 24 hours a day, year-round. Most accommodation is in single-sex dormitories. Private double rooms and family rooms are available. Very close to Molson Centre for hockey fans.
✚ E8 ✉ 1030 rue Mackay ☎ 843 3317 or 1 800/663 3317 Ⓜ Lucien l'Allier

MONTRÉAL
travel facts

ARRIVING & DEPARTING

Before you go

- Visitors from Scandinavia, the EU and most British Commonwealth countries require a full passport. UK and Irish visitors do not require a visa.

- Vaccinations are not required unless you are coming from a known infected area.

When to go

- June to October are the best months to visit Montréal, though long winters make nearby resorts attractive for skiers.

- Winters are long and bitterly cold – 10°C (14°F) on average in January, but as low as -20°C (-4°F). Late spring to early autumn is mainly temperate. July temperatures average 22°C (72°F) but can reach over 30°C (86°F).

Arriving by air

- Montréal has two airports: the Aéroport de Dorval ☎ 633 3105 22.5km southwest of the city, handles commercial flights; the Aéroport de Mirabel ☎ 476 3010 56km northwest of the city, handles chartered flights.

- Taxis to the city centre take 45 minutes from Mirabel, 25 minutes from Dorval. The Autocar Connaisseur shuttle buses ☎ 934 1222 are cheaper and very frequent. A shuttle service also operates between the two airports ⊙ Hourly 9:30PM–11:30AM and every 20 minutes 11:40AM–8PM. In the city centre, all buses drop off and pick up passengers outside the 'Aéroports' building of the Gare Centrale (on the corner of rue Mansfield and rue de la Gauchetière).

Arriving by train and bus

- American Amtrak ☎ 800/USA RAIL and Canadian VIA Rail ☎ 514/871 9395 or 800/361 5390 in Québec province, trains arrive at the Gare Centrale ✉ 895 rue de la Gauchetière Ouest

- Montréal's bus station, the Terminus Voyageur ✉ 505 boulevard de Maisonneuve Est ☎ 514/842 2281 handles services run by Greyhound (Canada), Orléans Express, Voyageur-Colonial (Ontario and Québec) and Vermont Transit (New York, Boston, and other destinations in New England).

Car rental

To rent a car in Montréal you must be 25 or over (21 if using a major credit card).

- Avis ✉ 1225 rue Metcalfe ☎ 866 7906 or 800/321 3652

- Budget ✉ Gare Centrale, 895 rue de la Gauchetière Ouest ☎ 866 7675; 938 1000 or 800/268 8970

- Hertz Canada ✉ 1475 rue Aylmer ☎ 842 8537 or 800/263 0678

- Thrifty-Québec ✉ 1600 rue Berri, Bureau 9 ☎ 845 5954 or 800/367 2277

- Tilden ✉ 1200 rue Stanley ☎ 878 2771 or 800/387 4747.

Airlines

- American Airlines ☎ toll-free 800/433 7300 in Canada and the US

- Air Canada ☎ toll-free 800/361 8620

- British Airways ☎ 287 9147 or 800/668 1050 in Québec province

- Canada 3000 ☎ 450/476 9500

- Delta ☎ 337 5520 or toll-free 800/361 1970 in Québec

- KLM ☎ 939 4040

- Lufthansa ☎ toll-free 800/563 5954

- Northwest ☎ toll-free 800/692 7000

- Royal Aviation ☎ 450/476 3800; toll-free 800/667 7692

- Sabena World Airlines ☎ toll-free 800/955 2000

- Swissair ☎ 879 9154; toll-free 800/267 9477
- US Airways ☎ toll-free 800/267 9477
- US Air ☎ toll-free 800/943 5436.

ESSENTIAL FACTS

Travel insurance

- Travel insurance is strongly recommended for all visitors to Canada.

Tourist information

- Montréal's main tourist office is the Centre Infotouriste ✉ 1001 Square-Dorchester ☎ 873 2015 or 800/363 7777 in Canada and the US ⏱ 1 Jun–first Mon in Sep: daily 8:30–7:30; first Mon in Sep–31 May: daily 9–5 🚇 Peel. There is a smaller tourist information office in Vieux-Montréal ✉ 174 rue Notre-Dame Est at the corner of Place Jacques-Cartier ☎ 873 2015 ⏱ Mid-May–first Mon in Sep: daily 9–7; first Mon in Sep–mid-May: daily 9–1, 2–5 and information kiosks at the Aéroport de Mirabel ⏱ Daily noon–2:30, 3–8 and Aéroport de Dorval ⏱ Daily 1–8.

Public holidays

- 1 January; Good Friday; Easter Monday; Victoria Day (Monday in mid-May); Québec Day (24 June); Canada Day (1 July); Labour Day (first Monday in September); Thanksgiving (second Monday in October); Remembrance Day (11 November); 25 December; 26 December.

Money matters

- Units of currency are the cent (¢) and the dollar ($1=100¢). Notes come in dollar denominations of 5; 10; 20; 50; 100; 500; 1,000. Coins are 1¢ (a penny or a 'sou'); 5¢ (a nickel or 'cinq sous'); 10¢ (a dime); 25¢ (a quarter or 'vingt-cinq sous'); 1 dollar; 2 dollars. The one-dollar is known by English speakers as a 'loonie' after the bird (a loon) on one face.

Women travellers

- Montréal's streets are considerably safer than those of most North American cities. However, parks, back streets and unlit areas should be avoided after dark.

Time

- Montréal is on Eastern Standard Time, five hours behind Britain. Clocks are moved forward one hour on the first Sunday of April and go back one hour on the last Sunday in October.

Electricity

- Current in Canada is 100 volts AC (60Hz).
- Plug adaptors will be needed for UK or European appliances to match two-prong plugs.

Opening and closing hours

- Shops: As a general rule, shops open between Monday and Friday from 9 or 9:30 to around 6, and from 9 to 5 on Saturdays. Some shops open on Sundays, usually between noon and 5. Malls, supermarkets, and department stores have longer hours, typically from Monday to Friday between 10 and 9; Saturdays from 10 to 6 and Sundays from noon to 5.
- Banks: These open from Monday to Friday between 9 and 4. Some larger banks open on Saturday mornings.
- Post offices: Monday to Friday from 8:30 to 5:30, and in some cases Saturday mornings.
- Museums, galleries, and other

89

attractions have summer and winter hours: summer runs from Victoria Day (mid-May) to Labour Day (early September). Many museums close on Mondays.

Sales tax

- You can reclaim GST (Goods and Services Tax) on accommodation and for goods taken out of the country (purchases of $100 and over).
- Keep receipts and complete the Goods and Services Tax Refund for Visitors form, available from retailers, duty-free shops, or Revenue Canada, Visitors' Rebate Program, Ottawa, Ontario K1A 1JS.
- You can apply for a TVQ (Québec Sales Tax) rebate on the same form, for goods and services such as accommodation and entertainment.

PUBLIC TRANSPORT

- Montréal's integrated transport system consists of more than 150 bus routes and a 65-station underground system known as the Métro. The Métro links up with about 30km of walkways in the Underground City.
- For details of general routes and tickets contact STCUM, the Société de Transport de la Communauté Urbaine de Montréal ☎ 288 6287 or 280 5666 🕓 Mon–Fri 7AM–11PM; Sat, Sun and public hols 8AM–10PM.

Métro and bus services

- The Métro is efficient, safe, clean and quiet (carriages run on rubber wheels). There are four colour-coded lines: orange, green, yellow and blue.

Coloured signs at stations indicate different lines and their direction by stating the terminus (end destination) of each line. Four key stations provide the main interchanges between lines: Berri-UQAM (orange, green, and yellow lines); Lionel Groulx (green and orange); Snowdon (blue and orange); Jean-Talon (blue and orange).

- Flat-fare one-way tickets valid on both buses and Métro are available singly or in a discounted booklet of six tickets known as a *carnet*. Tickets are available from Métro kiosks, station machines and independent retail outlets around the city.
- To buy a ticket on a bus from the driver you must have the exact fare as no change is given.
- A one-day or three-day tourist pass – *Carte touristique* (Tourist Card) – allows you to travel at will on buses or Métro. Both may be purchased from the tourist office or downtown hotels.
- A transfer system allows you to complete a Métro journey by bus (and vice-versa) at no extra cost. A transfer ticket (*correspondance*) is available from machines in the Métro, and valid for one hour. Bus-to-bus or bus-to-Métro transfers can be obtained from drivers as you board a bus. Métro transfers cannot be used to gain re-entry to the Métro.
- Orange, green, and yellow lines 🕓 Mon–Fri 5:30AM–1AM; Sat 5:30AM–1:30AM; Sun 5:30AM–2AM
- Blue line 🕓 Daily 5:30AM–11PM
- Most buses run until about 12:30AM, when a night service

takes over on 27 selected routes.

- The STCUM also operates two commuter train lines. One, leaving from Gare Windsor and the Vendôme Métro station runs a far west as Hudson and Regaud. The other runs north from Gare Centrale to Deux-Montagnes. Weekend service is sparse. Tickets are available from machines at stations, but all STCUM passes are good for travel within Zone 1 on both lines. Fares vary depending on distance.
- Free maps of the Métro are available from ticket kiosks. The best is the *Carte Réseau*, which shows the whole system.

Taxis

- Taxis can be found at stands outside main hotels, near the train station and at major junctions. They can be hailed on the street when the sign on the roof indicates they are free. A 10–15 per cent tip is normal. Cab companies include:
Co-op ☎ 725 9885
Diamond ☎ 273 6331
La Salle ☎ 277 2552.

MEDIA & COMMUNICATIONS

Telephones

- Local calls from phone boxes cost 25¢. That includes calls to all numbers in the 514 area code – all municipalities on the island of Montréal itself – and to some numbers in the surrounding 450 area code (in such off-island suburbs as Laval, Longueuil, and Brossard). The rest of the 450 area code and all other area codes are long distance and you

will need to dial 1 to get an operator to tell you how much money you need to make the connection. Thereafter, have plenty of 25¢ pieces on hand to continue the call. If you're calling a 450 number and you're not sure whether it is local or long distance, try dialling 1 before the number: you will either get through or you will get a recording telling you it is a local call.

- For international and long-distance calls, buy a Hello! Phone Pass, or find public phones that accept credit cards, or go to the Bell-Canada office ✉ Bureau Public, 700 rue de la Gauchetière Ouest on the corner of rue University 🕓 Mon–Fri 9–5 where you can phone and pay for your call afterwards.
- Direct dial phones, where calls are charged directly to your bill, are common in many hotels and motels. A surcharge is levied.
- Many organisations have 'toll-free' (free-phone) numbers, which can be recognised by their 800 or 888 or 877 prefix. Some operate only within a province, others anywhere in Canada, and a few from anywhere in North America.
- Reverse-charge or 'collect' calls can be made by dialling 0 for the operator.
- Enquiries for local numbers can be reached by dialling 411.
- For a number outside the area you are in, including toll-free numbers, dial 1, then the area code, followed by 555 1212.

International telephone codes

- To call abroad from Canada dial the country code, the area code minus its first zero and the

number required.
- Australia 011 61
- Denmark 011 45
- Germany 011 49
- Ireland 011 353
- Netherlands 011 31
- New Zealand 011 64
- South Africa 011 27
- Sweden 011 46
- United Kingdom 011 44.

Post

- Montréal's main post office is Postes Canada ✚ F8 ✉ 1025 rue St-Jacques near rue de la Cathédrale ☎ 283 2567 Ⓜ Bonaventure
- Smaller post offices are inside shops, department stores, and train stations displaying the Postes Canada signs.
- Stamps can be bought from post offices, the Centre Infotouriste in Square-Dorchester (▶ 89), news-stands, hotel vending machines, the train station and bus terminal, airports, convenience stores (*dépanneurs*), and many other retail outlets.
- Within Canada, postcards and letters up to 30g are 46¢; between 30g and 1kg, $3.75. Cards and letters to the US cost 55¢ up to 30g. Rates for other destinations are 95¢ up to 30g and $2.10 up to 100g.
- Letters sent *poste restante* should be sent to the main post office marked 'c/o General Delivery' or 'c/o Poste Restante'. State a collection date if possible, otherwise letters will be returned to the sender after 15 days. Take photo identification (passport, driver's license, etc) when collecting mail. Letters sent for collection in hotels should be marked 'Guest Mail, Hold for Arrival'.
- Telepost is a 24-hour, seven-days-a-week service whereby messages can be phoned to the nearest CN/CP Communications Public Message Centre (details from hotels or tourist offices) for a telegram-like delivery anywhere in Canada or the US the next day or sooner.

Newspapers, television & radio

- Canada's two national newspapers – *The Globe* and the *Mail and the National Post* – are published in Toronto, but are easily available in Montréal. The English-language daily is *The Montréal Gazette*. French dailies are *La Presse* and the tabloid *Journal de Montréal*; *Le Devoir* is the newspaper of the French-speaking Québécois intelligentsia. There is also a weekly news magazine, *Macleans*. Major American papers like the *New York Times*, *Washington Post*. and *US Today* are widely available on the day of publication. Some newsstands carry a wide selection of European newspapers (▶ 71 panel).
- Canada has three national television networks – the publicly owned Canadian Broadcasting Corporation (CBC), which broadcasts in English on Channel 6 and in French on Channel 2; CTV, whose local affiliate broadcasts on Channel 12; and Global on Channel 44. Most American networks are also available – ABC on 22, CBS on 3, NBC on 5, PBS on 33 or 57 and Fox on 44. Most hotels and motels have cable or satellite TV with

pay-station options.
• CBC Radio 1 at 88.5-FM offers
a variety of news and serious
public-affairs; while Radio 2
serves up classical music and
cultural programmes at 93.5-
FM. The best English station
for local news, talk and traffic
reports is CJAD at 800-AM and
the best French one is CKAC
at 730-AM.

EMERGENCIES

Precautions
• By North American standards,
Montréal is remarkably crime-
free. But it's wise to be safe.
Don't leave valuables or
luggage in cars, don't carry
around large quantities of cash,
and keep your passports and
credit cards in a pouch or money
belt. Avoid parks, the area by
the train station and other non-
commercial parts of the city
after dark. Leave valuables in a
hotel safe – or at home.

Emergency telephone numbers
• Police, fire, ambulance ☎ 911 or
dial 0 for the operator, who will
then connect you.
• Hospitals: Montréal General
Hospital ✉ 1650 Cedar ☎ 937 6011;
Royal Victoria Hospital ✉ 687
avenue Pine Ouest ☎ 842 1231;
Montréal Children's Hospital
✉ 2300 rue Tupper ☎ 934 4499 or 934
4400
• Lost property: bus or Métro
☎ 280 4637; taxis ☎ 280 6660
Elsewhere contact the MUC
Police ☎ 280 4636
• UK Consulate ✉ 1155 rue University
☎ 866 5863 Ⓜ McGill
• British Embassy ✉ 80 Elgin Street,
Ottawa ☎ 613/237 1530
• Irish Embassy ✉ 130 Albert Street,
Ottawa ☎ 613/233 6281.

Medical and dental treatment
• If you need a doctor, first
contact your hotel. Lists of
doctors are available from
consulates and in the Yellow
Pages, otherwise try the
Information and Referral
Centre ☎ 527 1375 Ⓒ Mon–Fri
8:30–4:45. Outside office hours,
contact the nearest hospital or
CLS (Centre local de service
communautaires) health clinic.
• For information about dental
treatment call the Ordre des
dentistes du Québec ☎ 875 8511.
There is a 24-hour dental clinic
at ✉ 3546 avenue Van Horne ☎ 342 4444
• For information about opticians
contact the Ordre des
Opticiens ☎ 288 7542
• Most over-the-counter
medicines can be bought at
pharmacies or 'drug stores'. If
you need medicine on a
prescription there are 24-hour
pharmacies at ✉ 5122 chemin de la
Côte-des-Neiges ☎ 738 8464 and ✉ 901
rue Ste-Catherine Est ☎ 842 4915. Bring a
prescription with you if you
need to renew any medicines.
This will avoid problems at
Customs and help the
pharmacist.

Useful telephone numbers
• American Express ☎ 284 3300 or
392 4422 Lost or stolen cards
☎ 281 9824
• MasterCard ☎ 877 8610 or toll-free
800/307 7309
• Visa ☎ 800/847 2911
• Road breakdown ☎ 800/CAA HELP or
861 1313
• Thomas Cook ☎ 398 0555 or 397
4029
• Touring Club de Montréal-
CAA-AAA-RAC ☎ 861 7111
• Weather ☎ 636 3026.

INDEX

CityPack
Montréal

Written by Tim Jepson
Edited, designed and produced by
        AA Publishing

Maps   © Automobile Association Developments Limited 1997, 2000
Fold-out map © RV Reise- und Verkehrsverlag Munich Stuttgart
        © Cartography: GeoData

Distributed in the United Kingdom by AA Publishing, Norfolk House, Priestley Road,
Basingstoke, Hampshire, RG24 9NY

The contents of this publication are believed correct at the time of printing. Nevertheless, the
publishers cannot be held responsible for any errors or omissions or for changes in the details
given in this guide or for the consequences of any reliance on the information provided by the
same. Assessments of attractions, hotels, restaurants and so forth are based upon the author's
own personal experience and, therefore, descriptions given in this guide necessarily contain an
element of subjective opinion which may not reflect the publishers' opinion or dictate a
reader's own experiences on another occasion.
We have tried to ensure accuracy in this guide, but things do change and we would be grateful
if readers would advise us of any inaccuracies they may encounter.

ISBN 0 7495 2352 2

Published by AA Publishing (a trading name of Automobile Association Developments
Limited, whose registered office is Norfolk House, Priestley Road, Basingstoke, Hampshire
RG24 9NY. Registered number 1878835).

Colour separation by Daylight Colour Art Pte Ltd, Singapore
Printed and bound by Dai Nippon Printing Co (Hong Kong) Ltd.

Acknowledgements
The Automobile Association would like to thank the following photographers, libraries
and associations for their assistance in the preparation of this book:
Allsport UK Ltd 13b; Canadian Centre for Architecture 32; Centre d'Histoire de
Montréal 39b; Imagos (C Coe) 44b; Musée des beaux-arts de Montréal 31b; Jean-
François Pin 8, 17, 42a, 44a; Reflexion phototheque 29 (Patricia Miller), 34a (M Gagné),
37a (Anne Gardon), 37b (Sean O'Neill), 51 (Michel Julien); Neil Setchfield 5b, 57
All remaining photographs were taken by Jean-François Pin and are held in the
Association's own library (AA Photolibrary).

Second edition revised by *Paul Waters*
Second edition updated by *Pitkin Unichrome Ltd.*
Indexer *Marie Lorimer*

Titles in the CityPack series